The Path to Fernglade

The Path to Fernglade

SUSAN HUMPHREY

WOODS EDGE PRESS

2020

ISBN: 978-0-578-61643-8

Copyedited by Pat Goudey O'Brien and Louise Watson
Text designed and composed by Dean Bornstein
Cover photo by Susan Humphrey

Published by Woods Edge Press, Weybridge, VT
woodsedgepress@gmail.com

To Drew, Phoebe, and Hadley, bright lights in the world.

And to Natalie, whose love knows no bounds.

Introduction

My husband, Gregg, and I are the parents of two sons, Andrew and Daniel Humphrey. This book is the story of how our younger son, Dan, was diagnosed with a rare cancer and died just a year and a half later. It is also the story of how I, along with the rest of our family, survived and, over time, came to love life again.

The book consists mainly of letters I wrote from 2007 through 2016. In the beginning the letters were mailed out fairly regularly and were relatively short. They informed friends how Dan was doing. Over time the letters became less frequent. They also became longer and were mostly about my own experiences. A few minor edits have been made here and there. The original letters were handwritten in my scrawled printing, and the postscripts were not just at the ends but often at the tops or even the sides, wherever there was room. More recently I have added narratives between the letters. Certain details and stories just begged to be included.

The cancer that developed in Dan is extremely rare. We were told that the chances of contracting this cancer are about the same as getting struck twice by lightning. And that is a bit how it felt. Out of the blue Dan was struck, and so was our whole family. It was shocking to the core. And yet, once the reality sank in, I did feel a power rise within me, what I call a "Mother force." I felt I could do this, whatever it was we were being called to do, we who journeyed by Dan's side.

Being an amateur photographer and in the habit of observing daily wonders, I slipped easily into the role of witness-observer. Yes, there was fear, sadness, and pain along the way. But there was also hope and great love. There was curiosity, too—this was uncharted territory.

I took endless photos and videos of Dan. I tried to scribble down all of the synchronicities and inexplicable coincidences when they occurred. I looked for and found a golden thread, what some might call the Hand of God or Mystery, weaving steadfastly in and out, blessing the path each step of the way.

After Dan died, I questioned whether anyone would still be interested in all of this. A friend encouraged me to keep going. "That which is most personal is also most universal," she said—a quote I later found attributed to Carl Rogers. And so I kept writing. For years.

We all experience sorrow, loss, and unwelcome change in our lives. Sometimes we are not sure we will make it through. But the human spirit is resilient, and the holy hides in the most unexpected of places. I hope sharing the story of this particular journey may gift you in ways beyond my knowing.

MOSS GLEN FALLS

2007–2009

. . . and the simple breath that kept him alive.

—Naomi Shihab Nye, "Kindness"

Kindness

Before you know what kindness really is
you must lose things,
feel the future dissolve in a moment
like salt in a weakened broth.
What you held in your hand,
what you counted and carefully saved,
all this must go so you know
how desolate the landscape can be
between the regions of kindness.
How you ride and ride
thinking the bus will never stop,
the passengers eating maize and chicken
will stare out the window forever.

Before you learn the tender gravity of kindness,
you must travel where the Indian in a white poncho
lies dead by the side of the road.
You must see how this could be you,
how he too was someone
who journeyed through the night with plans
and the simple breath that kept him alive.

Before you know kindness as the deepest thing inside,
you must know sorrow as the other deepest thing.
You must wake up with sorrow.
You must speak to it till your voice
catches the thread of all sorrows
and you see the size of the cloth.

Then it is only kindness that makes sense anymore,
only kindness that ties your shoes
and sends you out into the day to gaze at bread,
only kindness that raises its head
from the crowd of the world to say
It is I you have been looking for,
and then goes with you everywhere
like a shadow or a friend.

—*Naomi Shihab Nye*

In the spring of 2007, my son Dan was experiencing pain in his left calf muscle, and he noticed that it was slightly larger than the right calf. A healthy 24-year-old, he had been a ski and snowboard instructor at the Middlebury College Snow Bowl the previous winter, and he wondered if he had injured the leg. During lessons, he had often gone down the mountain backwards, in a snowplow position in front of his students, guiding them safely to the bottom. This technique put a lot of strain on his leg muscles.

Dan saw a physical therapist for several weeks, but there was no change. About the time she recommended an X-ray, he slipped while mowing the lawn and found himself in excruciating, yet inexplicable pain. The emergency room visit didn't turn up anything definitive. He was given crutches and advised to have further X-rays if things didn't improve.

After an MRI a few weeks later, the orthopedist's office called to postpone Dan's appointment for a couple of days. I found that reassuring news; it couldn't be that serious if they wanted to postpone the appointment. What I did not know was that often doctors don't look at scans until the day of the appointment. Dr. Benz, the orthopedist, had not yet seen the MRI results.

I was working as a part-time cashier at the local food co-op when I got a message to come to the front office to take a phone call. It was my husband, Gregg, who calmly told me I needed to come home. The doctor's office had called, Dan had a tumor in his calf, and we were to meet with Dr. Benz in his office that night, after hours. It was July 3, 2007. At the time, I remember a well-meaning co-worker trying to reassure me. But part of me knew, deep down, that something *big* was happening, and I felt the beginning of a seismic shift.

Dr. Benz showed us the MRI scans and explained what he saw. It was not good news. Because the next day was a holiday, Dr. Benz arranged an appointment for the day after that at Massachusetts General Hospital in Boston. Dr. Springfield, an orthopedic surgeon at Mass General with whom Dr. Benz had trained, was an expert in sarcomas—cancers of the connective tissue.

Gregg drove Dan and his girlfriend, Natalie, to Boston. They met with Dr. Springfield on July 5 and several more times over the following weeks. Dan's tumor was found to be an extraskeletal myxoid chondrosarcoma, a very rare cancer. The good news was that it is usually a very slow-growing cancer; the bad news was that there is no cure.

After one of the succeeding visits, Gregg had planned to call me to let me know what the next step would be. I was driving home from work, anticipating his call, when I stopped at a crosswalk in town. A young woman in shorts, holding an ice cream cone, was practically skipping across the street. She looked happy and full of life. It was only when I took a second look that I noticed one of her legs was a prosthetic. I recalled hearing several years earlier about a girl who had lost her leg in a bear attack. Here she was, on this particular day, crossing in front of me. It did not feel like a random event—it felt like I was meant to be there, watching her. I knew at that moment that Dan's leg would be amputated, too, and that it was the least of our worries. I think I might have prayed, "Take his leg, but please save his life."

Gregg called shortly after I got home. I said, "You don't have to tell me. I already know. They're going to amputate his leg."

A few days before the scheduled surgery, I decided on the spur of the moment to gather some friends together for a healing circle send-off. It was amazing how many came on such short notice. It was a beautiful Sunday afternoon in July and not beastly hot, thank goodness. I didn't have much planned, but we joined hands and I led everyone around our yard, snaking in and out of gardens and around trees. We often stopped to read a poem, say something, or just breathe together. Naomi Shihab Nye's "Kindness" and "Celtic Benediction" were two of the readings. I was carrying a length of orange silk cloth, and at one point I got the idea of going in and out of the circle, using the cloth to weave our love and prayers together. Then, just before breaking for refreshments, I brought out one of Dan's road bikes and put it in the middle of the circle. I wanted us to visualize him riding that bike again someday.

That Sunday afternoon, the day before Dan's leg was to be amputated, I felt the enormity of all that was ahead. I also felt the strength of friendship, and a profound connection to the spirit world—all that cannot be seen but is a very real presence and comfort in our lives. And that is how the letters began.

I did not have a computer in those years, so I sought an alternate way to keep friends and family abreast of Dan's journey. The first letter was mailed to those who had come to the gathering at our house. But over the years the circle grew; Dan had no idea there were so many out there in the world rooting for him. Praying for his life.

July 2007

Dear Healing Circle Friends,

I just want to thank each and every one of you for coming to our house last Sunday. Gathering such an amazing group of women friends together, well, it was just awesome. I can't imagine a better send-off for Dan and our family.

Not only did the power of your friendship travel with us to Boston (yes, I brought the orange silk along in our suitcase!), but I believe the impact of this day of sharing will be with me for many years ahead; in truth it is now a piece of my life's fabric. There were so many layers—stories told and untold, connections known and not yet known but felt, presences seen and unseen. I really can't thank you enough.

One unexpected gift for me was the resurrection of my teacher self! I know now that she is alive and well, though usually dormant. Sunday afternoon brought back memories of the classroom when so often we would share what I might call "holy" moments. I confess that teaching was always scary for me—but I would show up each day and feel my fear dissolve into love and connection, always with the help of the children. It is only now, looking back, that I wonder if that vulnerability, not my expertise, was the greater gift.

The operation went well! Angel Natalie has become Nurse Natalie, attending to Dan's every need with the most loving care. We met wonderful people in Boston, and Mass General Hospital became our home for a few days. Dan's operation was Monday afternoon and we left Friday morning. Dan is a strong fellow, and with the right prosthetics we really do believe he will be able to do just about anything he sets his mind and heart to. In the next few weeks we will probably find out if he needs chemo treatments. Please know how much I admire and love each of you.

In gratitude,
Susan/Susie/Sue

P.S. Dan's spirits are good—though at times he's in quite a bit of pain and has sad moments.

Celtic Benediction

Deep peace of the
Running Wave to you.

Deep peace of the
Flowing Air to you.

Deep peace of the
Quiet Earth to you.

Deep peace of the
Shining Stars to you.

Deep peace of the
Son of Peace to you.

—Anonymous

ONE NIGHT, not too long after the amputation, we were awakened by Dan's yelling. I didn't know what had set him off, but he was so angry and frustrated that he threw one of his crutches down the stairs.

We got him settled back in bed. He was sitting up, rocking, as he clutched his stump and sobbed. We rubbed his back and tried to say calming words. I realized that I had been so focused on the hope that the amputation might save his life that I had forgotten what a shock it must be to lose a limb. Something you were born with and lived with all your life, suddenly, inexplicably, gone.

Later Dan became convinced that part of his meltdown was due to the drugs. He had been leery of taking any pain medication. But I think the main cause was grief; he had a lot to grieve.

When we arrived home from Mass General Hospital, Gregg and Natalie took charge of the wound care. They had been shown exactly how to dress and wrap Dan's stump. Dan had not been allowed to leave the hospital until he could demonstrate that he was able to use crutches to walk up and down stairs and travel a good distance down a hallway.

Dan's hospital roommate was kind of wild but we all liked him. Dave was there due to a motorcycle accident. He really appreciated Dan and admired his courage and spirit. One time when Dan was in the bathroom, he told me so, and his eyes filled up with tears. He was a rough and rowdy guy on the outside, a teddy bear on the inside.

Sometimes I really did not know how to help Dan. The first few months after the amputation, he experienced a lot of "phantom" pain that he described as a feeling of being electrocuted. There were a few days early on when both Gregg and Nat were away visiting family. On one of these nights Dan was crying in pain and literally writhing. I finally understood what that word—writhing—really means. I don't remember what I did to try to relieve the pain, but nothing seemed to help. Finally I just sat in a chair at the foot of the bed, and watched and waited and prayed. After what felt like a long time, the writhing and moaning stopped, and Dan drifted off to sleep.

OUR OLDEST SON, Andy (almost four years older than Dan), his wife, Megan, and the grandkids visited that summer. Having little kids running around is exhausting, but it is also distracting and a great mood booster! Drew and Phoebe played often with Dan and Natalie. Nana's toy cupboard was a bottomless pit of interesting treasures, relics left over from when Andy and Dan were little boys.

I think Andy was trying to find some way to help. He and Megan decided our rather grubby downstairs bathroom was long overdue for a makeover. They came up with a plan to redo the floor, replace the toilet, paint the walls, and get new fixtures for the sink. They would do the work themselves, and they wanted to "surprise" me with their color choices, etc.

How could I not be grateful for such unexpected generosity? Yet I am quite fussy about my surroundings, and I don't like surprises! In fact, for the most part, I don't like change, even when it is often for the better. I was already anxious about Dan, and now I found myself worrying about what my "new" bathroom would look like. When they talked about painting the walls green, I managed to convince them to use a shade of yellow similar to what was already there. I decided to give up control when it came to everything else. A friend of ours helped Andy a bit with laying down the new vinyl tiles and installing the toilet. Andy and Megan did the work over a few days, and they were some of the hottest and most humid days of that summer. The next summer, a metal bar was added to the wall near the toilet; Dan's back was hurting by then, and the supportive bar helped.

Although I still don't really like the flooring, I somehow grew to love this bathroom. It now houses my collection of teacups, teapots, dessert plates, and flower vases. The various heights of my children and grandchildren are inscribed on the wooden trim around the door. Mostly I love it because it reminds me of Andy's wanting to help, and of his "I can figure out how to do this myself" attitude, so much a part of who he is. And it was definitely good for Dan to have a clean, cheery bathroom to use.

On AUGUST 27, just five weeks after the amputation, Dan and Natalie announced their engagement. I don't remember how I knew this was brewing, but I did help just a little by offering Dan an old family ring from my mother's side of the family. It had a gold band and a beautiful blue center sapphire with a diamond on either side. I knew it was probably fancier than Natalie would have liked, but I also knew she would appreciate its beauty and that it was a family heirloom.

That Monday afternoon in August, Dan and Nat took a little hike at the Middlebury College Snow Bowl, where Dan had taught Natalie how to snowboard. He was working on wearing the prosthetic leg but was still on crutches at that point, getting around pretty skillfully. He surprised Nat by taking a small blue leather box out of his backpack, getting down on his one good knee, and proposing to her.

She replied, "Of course!" Dan had terminal cancer, an uncertain future, only one leg, and no job. Without a moment's hesitation, Natalie said "Yes!" That's love.

There were many joys and sorrows ahead, but the greatest joy was Natalie. I would tell people that Dan had the best antidepressant out there, and it wasn't a pill. It was Natalie. When I first met her, long before Dan got cancer, I remember saying to a friend, "What is this angel doing in our lives?" Oddly enough, I didn't ask what this angel was doing in Dan's life. I said our lives. And so it came to pass that Natalie's healing and beautiful presence, combined with the love she and Dan shared, brightened and somehow made bearable even the darkest of times yet to come.

Not knowing whether the prosthetic leg would be covered under Dan's health insurance, Andy had an idea for a small fundraiser. He set up a website called One Leg Up, and Dan designed a t-shirt to sell, with one of his drawings on the front. Once we realized his insurance would cover most of the cost of the new leg, Dan stopped selling the shirts. But he kept track of the sales and personally thanked each buyer with the following letter:

Dear Friends,

Thank you so much for all you have given me in the past months. When I first found out that my left leg would be amputated, I didn't know what to expect. I never could have guessed that the local community would be so supportive in helping me to pay for medical bills and being beside me in spirit for this journey.

Since the operation I have progressed significantly from a state of severe phantom pain where I was barely sleeping to a more normal existence. Though I still miss not having my leg, this adversity has given me the opportunity to pursue career options that I may have been too intimidated to take on before the surgery. I am currently completing prerequisite classes at CCV for a career that will most likely be in Physical Therapy or Sports Medicine. I have also been working to support myself by teaching saxophone and piano in the community as well as working off and on at the Middlebury Natural Foods Co-op.

Again, I can't stress how much everybody's support has meant to me. I received my prosthetic leg a few months ago, and although

*walking has been extraordinarily difficult, I can now walk for
short periods without a cane. I have been keeping in shape by
swimming and I hope to be snowboarding by using a special
extreme-sports prosthetic by late January.*

Sincerely,
Dan

November 2007

Greetings to All!

*I confess, I've had the most wonderful Thanksgiving, and I've been
alone! I love my family dearly, but I've also noticed as I've gotten
older that some alone time is very nourishing to my soul. I've been
telling everyone that this Thanksgiving I've been on a gratitude
retreat. Gregg needed to help out his brother Tom, recovering from
heart surgery. Dan went to his fiancée's family. Andy and his family are in Traverse City, MI. So—just Buddy (dog) and I, keeping
cozy at home. It was a pretty decadent day…reading most of the
morning, knitting a vest for my grandson, not getting dressed until
5 p.m. (!) in time to go to a friend's house for a delicious feast. Feeling very happy, doing simple chores around the house.*

*For those of you who may not have heard…the news that tops
all the rest is our summer of cancer. In short, Dan had a calf muscle
bothering him for many months, an MRI in late June, an aggressive
cancerous tumor diagnosis in early July, and an above-the-knee
leg amputation a few weeks later. On the other side of the scales…
meet Natalie Guarin! An exceptionally kind, intelligent, beautiful
person. She and Dan are in love, they are engaged! Oh, what a
blessing!*

*Phoebe turned two, Drew turned four. My grandchildren are so
dear that I say being with them feels like a religious experience—
more holy, more spiritual, closer to God, than being in church or*

just about anything else. They have this aura of "goodness" (hard to describe) that must have been in us all at some point, probably still is—under all the layers. Innocence, vulnerability, sensitivity—they are just too sweet for words.

A helpful prayer that someone shared with me when Dan was first diagnosed goes like this—"Thank you, for everything, exactly the way it is right now."

Much love to you all,
Susan/Susie

ON THE FIRST REALLY beautiful spring day, mid-April 2008, I was working at the bookshop when I got a call from Dan. He wondered if I could possibly take him to Yankee Medical in Burlington, an hour's drive away, to see if someone there could adjust his prosthetic leg. He'd been trying to ride his bike that day, and something wasn't working right. I thought he had a lot of nerve and said something like, "Dan, I can't possibly take you today. I'm at work!"

Although clearly this was not an emergency, after I hung up I started to think more about it. It was really slow at the store that afternoon. The owner/manager was not around, but I asked my friend and co-worker Mary what she thought of my leaving early.

"Sure, why not?" So I called Dan back and told him I'd drive him up after all.

Our meeting with the technician didn't take long. Dan had brought his bike, and he demonstrated the problem. They went inside to adjust the prosthesis and were soon outside again. Propping the bike up against the building, Dan got on and took off down the sidewalk. He looked so good! At the end of the sidewalk, he turned left onto the road and pedaled out of sight without looking back.

I teared up, caught off-guard by an unexpected wave of emotion. I felt like a proud mother watching her child take his first steps. My heart swelled as Dan took flight, disappearing around the corner. We waited, and we waited some more. It seemed so quiet and still. Suddenly, there he was! At the opposite end of the block, he came full circle and pedaled towards us, strong and sure with an exultant grin on his face.

The old me would never have been able to be so "irresponsible" as to leave work early just to take my son to Burlington on a whim. There are many things in Dan's journey that I might do differently now, but on this day I made the right decision. Looking back, I realize that I did not have many opportunities for quality time alone with Dan during his illness; usually Nat or Gregg was with us. The drive home on this day was otherwise pretty ordinary, yet it remains a treasured memory. The Vermont landscape was so beautiful, coming to life after a long winter. The setting sun over the Adirondacks was warm and soft. And Dan was happy, filled with a childlike eagerness to start riding his bike again.

He called Nat on the way home to tell her about his success and to tell her we'd stopped at the Cheese Outlet, a little market on Pine Street, where he'd picked up some "yummies" for their supper. With all of the difficulties we'd been through so far and the uncertainties that lay ahead, to share this simple drive home, to sit contentedly with Dan next to me, happy and at peace, proved a blessed respite. Priceless.

May 2008

Dear Friends and Family,

I've really been looking forward to writing you all with an update on Dan's progress and life. I was planning to write you in June sometime. I wanted you to know that he's been doing amazingly well—teaching music, taking classes (A's, A+'s, and one A-!), teaching an advanced math group at Weybridge School a few hours a week, swimming at the college pool, and learning to bike again. He was looking forward to starting his graduate program at UVM this summer—a three-year Ph.D. program in physical therapy. He was looking forward to being able to help others. And Natalie was to start her nurse practitioner program. And the most important part of their day continues to be their time spent together—laughing, sharing, planning their future. Dan dreamed of a family someday. They would joke at how klutzy their kids would probably be—being that both Dan and Natalie can, at times, have problems with what we call "body, space, and time."

I am so sorry to be sharing with you some very sad news that has completely shocked us out of our minds. Dan had been experiencing some severe back pain, which we thought was most likely related to his prosthetic leg not fitting well any more (his stump had shrunk quite a bit), or perhaps, at the worst, that he had injured his back and had a herniated disk. Unfortunately that was not the case. After an MRI here in Middlebury and then further tests down in Boston yesterday (May 16), we have learned that Dan has at least three more tumors in his lower back that are most likely from his original cancer. We return to Boston on Monday to learn of the biopsy results. But it is most likely that Dan's original cancer has now spread.

This is the most shocking of news, and even though we've always known the cancer could return, we feel somehow blind-

sided. We thought it would show up first in his lungs, and his lung X-rays (taken every three months) continue to be clear of cancer. It was only when Dan described some severe pain (which only started about a week ago) that I began to worry that something could be going on.

We still don't know what all of this means, but it doesn't look good. It is not curable. The goal now is to proceed with radiation treatment and then chemo. The goal is to shrink the tumors (especially the largest one) and treat all of them so that Dan experiences less pain, a better quality of life, and hopefully a longer life. We don't really know how much time he is likely to have. Perhaps next week we will have a better idea. And there are always miracles that can happen.

There has been great sadness and many tears, needless to say. One thing I've always loved about Dan is his transparency—and how one minute he can seem so mature and adult, and the next minute he is my five-year-old Dan. Yes, he sobbed when he saw his dreams for his future being just washed away with this cancer diagnosis. And dear Natalie. If there is a god, or goddess, Natalie is surely heaven-sent. You cannot believe how amazing she is. She has certain qualities and a way of being that I find hard to put into words. Her very presence is enormously healing and uplifting to us all.

Last night, driving home from Boston and listening to Dan and Natalie cuddling and talking in the back seat, I thought to myself that if I get through this, it will be because of Natalie, because of the LOVE she shares with Dan. A friend gave me a little wall hanging last year that says, "Love bears all things, believes all things, hopes all things, endures all things." Dan and Natalie's love is like that. It is so powerful, it trumps the cancer. I feel certain that Dan and Natalie have been together before in a past life, and that they will indeed find each other again in some future life. It is their profound love for each other that will guide me in the days ahead—that will teach me and help me to know what to do to best support Dan for whatever amount of time is left for him to live. I pray that he will not be in too much pain—that he will have time to laugh, to be silly, to love. I hope he will feel all of our love and support.

This will most likely be the hardest thing I go through in my lifetime. In deepest sorrow, I am your friend,

Susan/Susie

P.S. Both Dan and Natalie will defer their graduate programs. Natalie is also leaving her job at the college so she can devote all of her time to Dan.

P.P.S. Needless to say, I would give anything to be able to change places with Dan.

I share with you a Mary Oliver poem I happened to come across on May 15 (just about the same time Dan was getting the MRI). It is from her new book, Red Bird.

Invitation

Oh do you have time
   to linger
      for just a little while
         out of your busy

and very important day
   for the goldfinches
      that have gathered
         in a field of thistles

for a musical battle,
   to see who can sing
      the highest note,
         or the lowest,

or the most expressive of mirth,
   or the most tender?
      Their strong, blunt beaks
         drink the air

as they strive
   melodiously
      not for your sake
         and not for mine

and not for the sake of winning
   but for sheer delight and gratitude—
      believe us, they say,
         it is a serious thing

just to be alive
  on this fresh morning
    in the broken world.
      I beg of you,

do not walk by
  without pausing
    to attend to this
      rather ridiculous performance.

It could mean something.
  It could mean everything.
    It could be what Rilke meant, when he wrote:
      You must change your life.

—*Mary Oliver*

THERE ARE A FEW particularly strong memories that stand out from the May visit to Mass General Hospital. One is of Dan playing piano. We stayed nearby at the Beacon House on Beacon Hill, where Gregg, Nat, and I had stayed during the amputation. The woman who managed the house was so friendly and welcoming. I imagined how hard her job must be; so many of her visitors, with whom she might grow close over the course of their treatments, she would never see again. Especially with sarcoma cancer, the odds are against you. I admired her sunny disposition, the steady and calm presence she exuded. There were several pianos in different rooms on different floors. I recall Dan finding and playing them all.

I have a short video clip on my computer that I have watched many times. It was taken at the hospital while we were waiting for Dan to have a CT scan before starting radiation the next day.

In it, Dan and Nat are sitting in the waiting room. They are being playful and silly, affectionate and tender. It is an intimate glimpse into the love they shared. If you listen carefully you can hear Dan say, "I love you so much, Natalie. I love you so much, Mom. Remember I love you both so much. Even if we don't make it through this, you've done so much for me and I really appreciate it."

Another strong image I carry from that time is of our meeting with the radiologist after the CT scan. We were back at the Beacon House. Dan was to start radiation the next day. I was in the bathroom when he received a call. A change of plans. The radiologist wanted to meet us that afternoon.

We met in the bowels of the hospital. A room down under, no windows. The lighting was harsh; it might have been fluorescent. The radiologist was a beautiful Asian woman. She had an aura of calm dignity tinged with a graceful sadness. She told us that the CT scan showed tumors in Dan's lungs. We had known all along that if tumors ever showed up in Dan's lungs, that would really signal the beginning of the end. We were stunned. Natalie and I immediately encircled Dan with our arms. The doctor may have slipped out. Dan was a deer caught in the headlights. We cried.

Later I stepped out to call Gregg. I was angry that he was not there with us. And I was angry that Dan was dying. The doctor recommended that Dan receive radiation closer to home. We headed back to Vermont.

A FEW DAYS BEFORE the radiation was to begin, Natalie called wondering if I wanted to go for a little drive with them. I was supposed to work at the Co-op, but any invitation to spend time with Dan and Nat was special indeed. First we went up to the Snow Bowl and had a picnic lunch not far from where Dan had proposed to Natalie. We walked a path through the woods to a clearing at the top of a hill. Beautiful wildflowers bloomed every-where along the way. I took a photo of Dan and Nat sitting in one of the chairlifts. Dan had grown up skiing and snowboarding on this mountain.

Then we headed over to Waitsfield, on the other side of the mountain. Dan talked a lot about biking on this road. I realized what a spiritual experience it was for him, biking alone along a stretch of many miles. At one point we stopped at a store for a snack. I chuckled watching how long it took Dan and Nat to decide on what they wanted, but what a good time they had in the process of choosing.

We also stopped at a beautiful waterfall, Moss Glen Falls. When I look at the pictures I took that day, I see vulnerability in Dan; he looks exposed. There is uncertainty in his eyes, maybe fear, too. But there is also courage and love. In Natalie, too, as she supports Dan with a tenderness that is as beautiful and delicate as the wildflowers we admired on the path. It is holy ground I am on, to be allowed a view into their souls as they were at that moment.

Although it was late May, it felt more like autumn. Dan was not saying it out loud, but I was aware that he was saying goodbye to places and memories that held special meaning for him.

Returning home via the Lincoln Gap, we had a small mishap on the way down. I can't remember what was wrong with the car, or how we resolved the problem. I just remember that we were pulled over to the side of the road for a while. I think smoke might have been coming from under the hood. And there was a bicycle tire hanging from a tree.

June 4, 2008

Dear Co-op Friends and Bookshop Friends,

Just checking in...a few of you have mentioned that you really like hearing from me. I'll try to keep you posted from time to time. On the good side, Dan was able to enjoy much of last weekend! He went to TWO performances at Jazz Fest and a dinner at the Black Sheep Bistro. Each day that Dan is able to enjoy brings me so much happiness. It's hard to describe. Oh—the things we take for granted.

On the not-so-good side, the last few days Dan has been experiencing more pain. The radiation treatments are coming to an end and the increased pain could be related to these treatments. Dan is now trying to decide which clinical study to be a part of. The doctor in Boston has described three different ones. He cannot recommend one over another, nor is he very optimistic about any of them. Remember, the goal here is not to cure the cancer, but to simply keep it in check for a little longer. Dan is trying to choose which study and will sign up for one of them by this coming Monday. The actual chemo will not start right away, giving him a bit of time to recover from the radiation.

Some good news is that none of the clinical trials will require an extended stay in Boston. He might go down for a day once a week, or something like that. That is a relief. Also, there is a possibility of taking Dan to Maine for a little holiday before the treatment starts, if he feels up to it.

We're all holding up as best as we can, each in our own way. We are totally on some kind of journey—it's all unknown. One day at a time, as they say. I know when Dan feels increased pain, or pain in a new area, it brings up fear. I think that's one thing I hope the most for—that Dan not be in too much fear. Maybe that's where all the love will come in...to soothe the fear.

I am at times in tears because of the incredible support we have been receiving from so many, many people. Such goodness just breaks open my heart. Thank you for being there.

Love,

Susan

P.S. Attached is a poem by Mark Belletini that I happened to come across on May 31. It was in a Unitarian Universalist magazine I should not be receiving anymore, so when it arrived in the mail, I figured there was surely something in it that I was meant to read.

Reading for the Day

Let the sky above me unroll like a scroll,
and let me read upon it today's text for my life:
    "You are alive, here and now.
        Love boldly and always tell the truth."

Let the wind arrange the naked branches
of the maples and aspens and oaks
into letters which proclaim this sacred text:
    "Your heart beats now,
        not tomorrow or yesterday.
        Love the gift of your life and do no harm."

Let the eyes and hands and faces
of all men and women and children
with whom I share this earth
be chapter and verse in this great scripture text:

"Life is struggle and loss, and also
tenderness and joy.
Live all of your life, not just part of it."

And now let all the poems and scriptures and novels and
films and songs and cries and lullabies and prayers and
anthems open up before our free hearts. Let them open like a
torah, like a psalm, like a gospel, like an apocalypse
and let them proclaim:
  "Do not think you can take away
  each other's troubles,
  but try to be with each other in them.
  Remember that you are part, not all,
  great, but not by far the greatest,
  small, precious brief breaths
  in the great whirlwind of creation."
And remember that every single human word is finally and
divinely cradled in the strong and secure arms of Silence.

—*Mark Belletini*

July 4, 2008

Dear Healing Circle Friends,

*It has been a year since that dreadful Tuesday—July 3, 2007—
when Dr. Benz told us that Dan's MRI showed a large sarcoma
tumor in his calf. I want you to know, my Healing Circle Friends,
that though we may not be able to save Dan's physical life, I
do believe we are doing powerful healing work on many levels.
I thank you all deeply for all that you have given to me, Dan,
Natalie, our whole family over this past year. And it just seems*

to continue...such an amazing outpouring of support—financial, nourishing food, prayers, comfort, company, it just goes on and on. I am so very grateful to you all.

We continue to be realistic while also being hopeful. Sometimes I am just surprisingly fine. Dan too. Other times it just takes the smallest thought to put me in tears. We try to live pretty moment-to-moment, enjoy the now, rather than ruining it by thinking of tomorrow. And of course, I still don't know how I will be, as time goes on. Who knows? I really don't worry about how I will be because I have total faith in you, my friends, to hold me up if I should really "lose it," as they say. And some of the time, every now and then, I've even had the feeling that as awful as this situation may be (I could even call it "horrific"), sometimes I feel that all is exactly as it is meant to be. Could that be possible? That all of my life, all those seemingly insignificant moments and encounters with so many different people, that they have led up to, and even prepared me for this moment in my life? Weird, eh?

At a soul level, who knows what it is we agree to do in this incarnation? So much is a mystery, including why someone like Dan (young, with a healthy lifestyle, and a good person!) would even get this very rare, incurable form of cancer. And I am reminded that most of what is going on is really out of my control. So I come back to each day asking myself, what is it today that I can do to be helpful? What is my part, however small, in this unfolding? I still have faith in some greater wisdom. I am not capable of seeing even a fraction of the truly bigger picture. Therefore, why not have faith in a greater wisdom? In a love beyond my understanding? Why not?

Speaking of love...Dan and Natalie still talk of marrying! They went yesterday to Autumn Gold to look at wedding bands. They found out that Autumn Gold will take an old gold bracelet of my mother's (it's stretched, so it is unwearable at present). The money from the bracelet will basically pay for two rings. I love the sym-

bolism of taking something old, from the past, to make something new. Transformation. I think how pleased my mother would be. I wish I knew more about the bracelet. It is one she wore a lot. It could have been an anniversary present for all I know. I think my father brought it back from Egypt.

Dan got a buzz haircut before his first chemo treatment. I think he's beginning to lose his hair. I suspect he'll lose most of it, eyebrows etc., too, after the next round. The chemo treatment involves a four-day stay at Fletcher Allen in Burlington. After this next chemo treatment, the doctors will reevaluate and either continue this one or try something new, if this one doesn't seem to be effective. I suspect that when/if Dan and Natalie do get around to "tying the knot," Dan will probably be pretty funny-looking by then. It is very reassuring knowing that no matter how strange, even possibly ugly-looking Dan becomes, his Natalie will still see him as totally handsome and lovable! He is one lucky guy in that department.

The other night Dan had a dream in which he was playing Magic the Gathering with old friends from elementary school. The next morning Dan went into his closet and pulled out all his old cards that he hasn't touched since about sixth grade. He's been sorting them, and making two decks, and teaching Natalie the game so they can play together. One of the kids in his dream was Matt Kireker, whom he hasn't talked to in about 10 years. A couple of days after the dream, Dan checks his email, and there is a long letter from Matt! The world works in mysterious ways.

Thank you <u>so</u> much for being there for, and with, me.

Blessed be,
Susan/Susie

ONE THING I FEEL good about is that, although Gregg and I were with Dan every step of the way throughout his illness, we did not try to smother him with love or to take over his life. We were happy to take a back seat most of the time and let Dan be the one in charge. Dan with Natalie first, and then Gregg and I, close behind, helping as he needed and wanted.

Sometimes it was a tricky balancing act. Once we found out the cancer had reached Dan's lungs, I really knew time was of the essence. What did Dan want to do with whatever time was left to him? I had observed Dan and Natalie making decisions together and often found the process painstakingly slow. The trick for me was to be a "nudger," to keep things moving along, while at the same time not becoming the one in charge. I tried to be an encourager, a reminder, and at times a sweeper of the path, so that the steps forward would continue at a steady pace. For lest we forget, a clock was ticking. Time was precious, precious indeed.

July 25, 2008

Dear Friends,

So much to write. I won't be able to include it all. I'll have to be thoughtful and precise in my choice of words, which, as you know, will be hard for me; I like to meander in my writing.

The most important news is that Dan and Natalie got married! Hurray! They were married in the Catholic church in Natalie's hometown of Millbrook, NY, on July 16, which is also the wedding anniversary of Natalie's parents and grandparents. On July 10 (Thursday) when Dan found out he had pneumonia, they stopped at a bridal shop in Burlington on the way home, and Dan bought Natalie a beautiful wedding dress (on sale, 40 percent off!).

On Saturday, July 12, they weighed the pros and cons of getting married that week…before Dan would lose all of his hair. Natalie was sad that Drew and Phoebe (Andy and Megan's little ones, ages four and two) would not be there; we checked online, but the airfares were far too expensive, but then Megan said she'd drive! Andy was in Boston. Megan drove by herself with the little ones from Traverse City, MI. Once Megan said she'd drive, Natalie said "yes"—7/16 would be the day.

There are so many details I will tell you at a later date, on how everything fell into place in just a few days' time. When you see the photos you will think that months of planning went into this wedding, except there was no time to hire a photographer. But we got some pretty good shots, nonetheless. And Dan did amazingly well on that day (recovering from pneumonia/pleuritis and also he had small blood clots we were not aware of at the time). I think he was just SO HAPPY that he really rallied for a long day. And he slept very well his first night as a married man.

All of the immediate family were there, as well as Natalie's "abuela" (grandmother on father's side) and a few friends. One of Natalie's friends played the organ. Phoebe was the flower girl and Drew the ring bearer. I think we were 18 for the dinner that night. They hope to have a big party in Vermont at a later date.

Dan started his second chemo treatment this past week. They had to delay a day when they discovered he had blood clots. He is given a shot in the tummy to thin his blood. Natalie has been taught how to do it. We joke that she deferred from the Nurse Practitioner Program but that instead, she is practicing nursing on Dan. Mid-August we should find out if this chemo treatment is working. Thanks again for all!

Love,
Me

P.S. I am writing from Fletcher Allen Hospital; Dan should be coming home today.

P.P.S. Natalie was positively RADIANT on her wedding day!

P.P.P.S. Dan and Natalie are looking to live by themselves somewhere nearby. They have a couple of possibilities to look into. Anyway, if you hear of someplace, reasonably priced (ha!), please do let us know. We're all getting along great; I just think they'd like to be on their own for a little bit. Thanks for keeping your ears open to what might be out there.

It is hard to believe that this beautiful wedding was put together in less than a week's time. Once Megan said she could drive with the kids from Michigan, and Andy could drive up from work in Boston, then it was full speed ahead.

I had had one of my imaginary conversations with God earlier in the week. I think I was asking for a little help. In my mind, God said, "I'm really very sorry about this cancer thing. There's a lot more going on than you can possibly know or understand at this time, with your limited human perspective. But the wedding? I just might be able to pull a few strings and help you out there." And that was, indeed, how it went.

Because Dan was in the process of selling one of his beloved road bikes, he had the money to buy Natalie a gorgeous wedding gown from the shop Sewly Yours. Even though it was on sale, it still cost over $1,000. Dan and Natalie were extremely frugal, so it delighted me no end that they would splurge in this manner. Dan called on the way home to tell me about the unexpected purchase. I asked, "How does she look in it?"

"Oh Mom," he said, "She looks beautiful. She looks like a model!"

Since Natalie is Catholic, she and Dan had to get special dispensation in order to marry on such short notice. They met with the kind priest at St. Joseph's Church, who gave them his blessing. They ordered the wedding cake and found a charming cake topper, circa 1950s. It depicted a bride and groom dancing together.

Dan's hair had started to fall out, but he still had most of it. He looked quite dashing in a rented black tuxedo with a blue bowtie, the blue tie being his one request. Natalie was, of course, the star, as all brides should be. She looked absolutely stunning in her elegant wedding gown with its exquisite detailing of barely noticeable seed pearls stitched along the empire waist, and also where the shoulder straps joined the bodice. That morning, Natalie had gone to a hairdresser who had swept back her glossy dark hair into a low chignon, partially held in place by a large barrette of pearls I had given her. Hanging from her earlobes were sparkling blue topaz earrings, a gift from Natalie's abuela.

I brought flowers from our garden and Megan made Natalie and Phoebe matching crowns of pink roses from a local florist. Natalie's bouquet was made of the same roses.

Drew was such a handsome and serious ring bearer in his white button-down shirt, brick-colored pants, and striped silk tie. He stood solemnly, holding the rings on a little white satin pillow. Phoebe was like a fairy child! With her curly hair and impish smile, she seemed to be in a world of her own as she twirled down the aisle sprinkling rose petals here and there. The regular priest was on vacation, but the visiting priest was a wonderful tall black man from Africa. He had presence and a rich, sonorous voice.

After the ceremony and picture taking, we went back to Natalie's family home for wedding cake, champagne, and hors d'oeuvres. I was grateful for the central air conditioning, as the sunny day had become quite warm and humid. Later in the evening we drove to nearby Rhinebeck, New York, for a gourmet dinner at the Beekman Arms Inn, a famous historic tavern. Dan and Natalie stayed there for the night while the rest of us returned to Millbrook or other destinations.

I know that under other circumstances, Dan and Natalie would have invited more family and friends. But considering that Dan had cancer and was in between chemo treatments, putting together a wedding on such short notice and having it all flow so smoothly, with reverence, laughter, and love, well, it was remarkable. Quite remarkable.

I'M NOT SURE EXACTLY when it was that Dan switched over to Dana Farber. He and Natalie were constantly researching his form of cancer and all the possible paths toward healing—from ingesting certain spices bought at the Co-op to looking into clinical trials as far away as Texas. Natalie had a friend with cancer who had been successfully treated at Dana Farber. Mass General had been very good to Dan, but at some point it seemed time to take a new direction. Dan really liked his new doctor.

September 5, 2008

Dear Friends,

I have been thinking of you so much and feel a letter is long over-due. It's just that whenever I'd get ready to write, some distraction would come along. Even now, I am trying to sneak this letter in between grandchildren resting/napping. (Andy, Megan, Drew, and Phoebe are visiting.)

I have had so many conversations with you in my head. So much gratitude. I have been thinking about my original family and how, in spite of some dysfunctional aspects (and who doesn't have that in their family of origin?), I do believe I managed to come out relatively unscathed. I think for the most part, I somehow did feel loved and lovable. Of course there were moments of shame and sadness, disconnection, loss, abandonment, and all the rest. But I am grateful that by and large, when family members behaved oddly, and even at times cruelly, I didn't take it personally. I accepted that most of the time, everyone was doing about the best that he/she could. I loved them anyway, while at the same time, I paid attention to who felt "safe" on any given day.

Which brings me to friends. I've been thinking about the role of friends in my life. My friends were, and are, my chosen family. And I hope when I die, if there's a service, someone stands up and says, "Susan had amazing friends." I look back now, and wonder if my mother consciously helped me with this at an early age. I believe she was rather shy as a child, and lonely at times. And maybe she wanted it to be different for me? Very early on I remember her helping me to connect with others, to be able to make friends: e.g., when we moved back from the West Indies (I was 12 years old), I met my next-door neighbor, Liz—but I'd already heard about her through my mom. I think I might even have written to her (from my boarding school). I couldn't wait to meet her.

My family at times could be a bit scary, but from four years old on, I always had one best friend who was really like a sister to me, and someone I could depend on. When I married Gregg, this dynamic changed, and there was a little sadness/feeling of loss around this, as I recall. Gregg became my best friend, really.

As time went on, and especially after I stopped teaching and had more time to devote to friendship, I became friends with many different people. I want you to know that I lit a candle in church several weeks ago and thanked you all. I said something like, "If one's wealth could be measured by the quality of one's friendships, then I am blessed to be very wealthy indeed!" And

*I feel grateful, just about every day, for you all. I have very few
original family members left—just one brother (I am the youngest
of six). I know he cares a lot for me and Dan, and yet not once
(in about a year?) has he talked to Dan on the phone (though he
calls me) or written him, or in any way even acknowledged his
marriage to Natalie. Yet I know he is very fond of Dan; my family
often had rather odd ways of showing their affection.*

*But I have a huge family, it turns out. My family of friends. You
are the best, and I love you dearly.*

Here is the latest Dan summary:

1. *The chemo didn't work. The lung tumors are growing quickly.
   The oncologist said we could be in serious trouble in as little as
   two months (that was two weeks ago or so).*
2. *Dan was excited to start a clinical trial, but at the last moment
   he didn't qualify when they discovered a spot in his brain that
   could be cancer.*
3. *Instead—he is now taking a drug called rapamycin (with very
   few side effects).*
4. *If the rapamycin is determined not to be effective, he might be
   able to start the clinical trial in about a month, if the spot in
   his brain turns out not to be cancer. Or he can try some other
   drug/treatment.*
5. *Most of the time he's feeling pretty good…occasionally he has
   some difficulty breathing. He and Natalie continue to be totally
   amazing in their positive attitude. I gave them a wedding present of a print (framed) titled "It's going to be a good day." It
   reminded me of Dan and Natalie because that's what they do.
   They are always choosing to have a good day.*
6. *They have a sweet apartment in town. A six-month rental just
   two doors down from their old apartment.*
7. *Dan often goes swimming at the college pool, and now that the
   effects of chemo are wearing off, he really enjoys good food.*

8. He has recorded songs on his keyboard to make into a CD!

Love to you all and thanks,
Susan

ANOTHER GOAL ON Dan's wish list was to make a CD of jazz songs he would play and record on his keyboard. Music was such a big part of Dan's life.

My mother had played piano, and I took some lessons when I was little. I wanted my boys to have the opportunity to play an instrument. In the late 1980s I was thinking it would be lovely to have a piano, but I didn't want to invest much money in buying one because I didn't know if either boy would be interested. I remember just gently "throwing it out to the universe" to send a piano.

Not long after, I was at a friend's house and I overheard her on the phone talking about trying to get rid of her piano. I said, "Betty, I've been wanting a piano!" She told me it could no longer be tuned and she wanted to just give it to me for free. But I insisted on paying her something, so $25 later we had our piano.

The first year it sat there. Andy rarely touched it, but Dan fooled around on it now and then. After that year I said, "Dan, you've shown an interest in the piano, so you get to have lessons!" He started taking piano lessons soon after, and from then on music became a source of comfort, joy, and inspiration in Dan's life.

In the summer (spring?) of 2008, Gregg's brother "Uncle Tom" sent away for and had shipped to Dan a beautiful high-quality keyboard, a Roland. Dan was thrilled. Interestingly, at times when he was experiencing pain in his leg (the one that wasn't there), he could play the keyboard and the pain would magically disappear, or at least greatly soften. How amazing that making music could somehow affect the wires in Dan's brain, and his experience of pain changed. Was it simply a distraction or something more? At any rate, it was better than drugs, with no harmful side effects.

Dan continued to teach just a few piano students: brothers Caetano and Marcelo (whom he'd also taught at Weybridge Elementary School) and Elizabeth from Middlebury. He was so proud of their progress.

What songs would Dan choose for his CD? A few were ones he wrote himself: "Once," "Lost," "Away," and even one called "Here Comes Natalie." When I listen to the CD, I sense Dan in conversation with the Universe. A few of the songs he wrote feel wistful, as though he is asking who or what is out there. Are you there, God? But most of the songs he chose to play were those of his musical hero, Dave Brubeck.

BACK IN 1999, when Dan was a sophomore in high school, Gregg bought tickets for the two of them to go hear Dave Brubeck play in Montreal. Dan was not all that thrilled to go hear some old man playing piano. But he came back from that concert transformed. He couldn't say enough good things about this musical genius, and from then on, Dave Brubeck became a role model for Dan. He hoped to have that same vigor, youthful passion, and joy in his twilight years. Dan started listening to a lot of Brubeck's music and playing some of his pieces too. He even wrote a short essay about him and included it in his college applications.

About that time, quite by chance, I met someone who had worked for Brubeck in Connecticut and was a personal friend of his. We secretly hatched a plan. Unbeknownst to Dan, my friend arranged for Dan's essay to be sent to and read by Dave. He wrote on it and sent it back with a beautiful black and white signed photograph of himself. At the end of the essay, Dan had written, "I have had recurring dreams of this jazz legend for the past two years. In my dreams I meet Brubeck after a concert and he teaches me piano. He shows me how to play inverted 7th major triads and augmented 9ths. I never want to wake up." What Dave wrote on the bottom of the essay was, "Dear Dan don't wake up Dave."

That's what we gave Dan for his graduation present—the returned essay with Brubeck's comment on it, along with the photograph. Dan was stunned and thrilled with this surprise. We framed the essay and photograph together and it still hangs on the wall on the stairs going up to his bedroom. Dan had a friend who received $2,001 as his graduation present, but Dan thought he'd gotten the best present of all.

And one night in June of 2008, Dan's dream wish came true. Dave Brubeck was playing in Burlington. My friend arranged for Dan and Natalie to go backstage and meet him and his wife, Iola, after the concert. They talked about music for a long time while Brubeck snacked on chips. For Dan, it was the thrill of a lifetime.

The bass player in Gregg's bluegrass band, Snake Mt. Bluegrass, had a recording studio in his home. That fall he was able to take the recordings from Dan's keyboard and make them into a CD, which Dan titled *Once*. Now Dan had something of his own creation that he could give to others. (To listen to the CD, go to https://youtu.be/19cqmXrcOAw.)

October 26, 2008

Dear Friends,

I think it's been quite a long time since I last wrote, but it doesn't feel like it to me because I am having conversations with you, in my head, on a daily basis.

I can't remember where I last left off, so please forgive me if there are some gaps. The short story is that Dan was able to qualify for the clinical trial in Boston that interested him several months ago. It is called AUY 922 Heat Shock Protein Infusion. He goes down to Boston every week for this infusion. We don't know yet how effective this treatment will be but we are hopeful. The doctor in charge of the trial (Phase I) is very reassuring and optimistic. Dan feels grateful to be in his care as well as all the other really great folks at Dana Farber. And the side effects don't seem too bad—nausea and diarrhea, but it wears off after a few days. He starts to feel pretty darn good just about at the time he starts the next infusion. Anyway—it's definitely a gentler treatment than the first chemo treatment he did at Fletcher Allen, in Burlington. And his hair is growing back! Very soft, like baby hair.

Looking back over this past month I can think of a few things to share with you. On several occasions, I've recognized that I was feeling happy. And then I'd think, "Isn't that the strangest thing? I have a son dying of cancer and I'm feeling happy." Well, first of all, we still have hope and we still have DAN! So sometimes, not looking backwards or forwards, I am just happy and grateful that Dan is still with us, sharing his "Dan" essence.

This past week I went to Boston with them and got to experience a little bit of their weekly routine. I just love being a "fly on the wall" around them. I don't think I do much that's very helpful, but I also try not to get in the way, either. They are just so much fun for me to be around is all I can say. There is a lot of laughing. Dan can be very silly, and Natalie just seems to totally appreciate this side of him. I love that they are both smart, intellectually curious, caring people, while at the same time they are often like little kids. It is really so dear, and my heart always opens when I am around to witness this side of their relationship. It is an honor. I know I'm blessed.

Another thing that happened this month was realizing the

41

importance of one's routines, and also the importance of some-
times letting go of those habits. The routines are grounding, reas-
suring, etc. But also they can act as blinders, and one can miss
out on opportunities and/or other ways of looking at things if one
simply sticks to one's usual habits and routines.

Because of somehow, luckily, paying attention, I ended up tak-
ing a quick trip with Dan and Nat to Millbrook, NY, where Nat's
family lives. The next day, there we were (me, Dan, Natalie, and
her parents) at St. Matthew's Church cemetery in Bedford, where
my parents and other family members are buried. I had not been
there since 1991, when my mother died. It was a short, but import-
ant visit. Definitely felt very significant to me, and I am so glad it
was Natalie's parents who got me there. It was a reminder that I
am being taken care of in ways beyond my understanding.

Two of my neighbors are moving out of Weybridge and into
Middlebury, and right next to each other! This has certainly
added to my feeling of the ground shifting under and around me.
Especially my neighbors right next door who have lived here as
long as we have. They will always be my neighbors, even after they
move. I have reflected on this idea of moving because I, too, some-
times think about moving. But I realize I am not ready to do this
anytime soon. Many times over the past few months I have felt
especially grateful for my house (not too big, not too small) in the
country. When I was little, I remember loving that picture book,
The Little House, *by Virginia Burton. At times I simply delight in*
how the sunlight comes through the windows, the warmth of the
wood stove, the comfort and security I receive from this imperfect
but strong little house. Thank you dear house, and forgive me for
complaining over the years about this or that minor flaw.

Going through my Co-op register line recently, my dentist's wife
looked me straight in the eye and said emphatically, "You need to
know, you're not missing anything." They love to travel and had
just gotten back from one of their favorite places, southern France.

One reason they like to travel is it makes them appreciate more deeply living in Vermont. It felt important to be reminded that staying put is often just fine, more than fine. I'm not missing anything, and I'm darn lucky to live where I do.

On November 26, Dan will be 26! This is his "golden" birthday (when you become the age of the day of your birth). A friend's daughter calls it your "lucky" birthday. I think it would be fun to surprise Dan with birthday cards from far and near, don't you? If you feel like sending a card, his address is: 106 South Main St., Apt. #3, Middlebury, VT 05753.

May your hearts be nourished by this soulful time of year!

Love,

Me

P.S. Gregg is doing well. He was able to spend five days in Maine for some much-deserved R & R. Golf at his favorite golf course, etc. He came back home in such good spirits, with renewed energy.

THERE WAS ONE AFTERNOON when Gregg was working at the College and I was hanging out with Dan and Nat at their apartment. It was snowing lightly outside, and everything was so peaceful and calm. I had missed an episode from one of my favorite "escape" TV shows, *Survivor.* Natalie said she could probably get it to play on her computer. My memory is that we each had a mug of tea, and that Dan, Nat, and I huddled together on their queen-sized bed and watched that silly program. For that hour I simply let go of the nightmare reality we were in. I remember being incredibly content, thinking, "Does it get any better than this?" Dan seemed not to be in pain, we were nestled together on a cozy bed and—if only briefly—lifted above the churning waters. A time out of time.

November 15, 2008

Dear Friends,

The Heat Shock Protein Infusion was not a successful treatment for Dan. He will have about a month off from any treatment and then start a new clinical trial.

This news was very discouraging, and even more disheartening is the fact that Dan is feeling worse. His back is bothering him more, as well as pain in his chest. The radiation he had in June on his back really did help, but they cannot radiate the same place again, unfortunately.

It was both a joy and a sadness to be with Dan and Nat on this last trip to Boston. It is still such a treat for me to be a witness to their love. They talk about everything. And they are still silly and goofy at times. And they are also sad. Dan is still somewhat bewildered, I would say, as to how this could even be happening to him. It's just a living nightmare. And dear Natalie, so positive and encouraging to Dan. And sometimes there are just no words between them—a deep sadness and love. They hug a lot.

I am not sleeping very well these days. I guess that's to be expected. Sometimes I feel breathless in the middle of the night. I am sure it is just anxiety. Again, thank you for being there, if I should lose my mind. Hopefully not.

In the middle of the sadness I am able to find something to be grateful for. I've noticed that even in my saddest moments, I am still able to feel connected to something—call it God, Source, Love, whatever. I am so very grateful for this because there was a time in my life when I inexplicably lost this connection and it was truly the most terrifying experience.

If my connection can remain intact, I feel more hopeful that I will be able to survive whatever is ahead. Being able to write you

*affirms this connection because really, it is the God in me writing
to the God in you, isn't it?*

*With time off before the next treatment, Dan and Natalie are
hoping to take a trip to a warm climate. And then be back home
for his birthday and Thanksgiving.*

Take care,
Love, Me

*P.S. Does anyone know how to get rid of red squirrels? There are
several living under our roof (crawl space above ceilings). They
wake me up, and I also worry that they are seriously damaging our
house. We would pay someone to help us get rid of them. Whom
to call?*

THANKS TO THE KINDNESS of neighbors, Dan and Natalie were
offered a free place to stay on the island of St. John during the first
week of December. It would be their honeymoon, and Nat's mom
and I were invited to go along with them!

It was a very special week. The best part was that Dan felt better in the warmer climate—he could breathe more easily. I was
chosen to be the designated driver, and I am proud to say I rose
to the occasion. Even for the best of drivers, it is not easy nav-
igating some of those nightmarishly steep winding roads and
hairpin turns, the likes of which you really have to see to believe.
They truly are scary. But there was no limit to what we could
and would do to be of service to Dan and Nat, and I knew some
greater power was helping me along the way.

Every day we chose a different beach to explore. I remember
snorkeling at one in particular. When I put my head under the
water, I entered a completely different world. It was a true escape.

The only sound was my breathing, and the sunlight flickered through from above, catching the scales of fish and the shapes of sea life. It was ethereal, and I sensed being in some other existence altogether.

At another beach, Dan found a beautiful shell with a hole in the top of it. He secretly passed it to me for safekeeping and asked if I could find a silk cord for it when we got back home. He wanted to make it into a necklace to surprise Natalie with a special Christmas present.

I took photos constantly and later made them into a honeymoon album. I wanted to capture every single bit of Dan and his life, because I knew he was leaving. I remember at one point taking a photo of Dan, looking at it on my camera screen, and wondering if it would be a good shot for his obit. Yes, one could see the port on his chest where the chemo liquid was administered, but I figured we could probably crop that out. Of course I said nothing of this to Dan. It turns out it was the one we chose.

The only unsettling event of the week was somewhere near the end of the trip. Dan and Nat had a bit of a tiff. It was pretty much the only disharmony I ever witnessed in their relationship, though there must have been other occasions. I don't know what had been said to have brought this on, but it didn't last very long. Even this I was grateful for, because in any marriage there will be moments of discord; I was glad Dan lived long enough to experience this, too.

The last night we were there, there was a free concert in town—a woman singing with a jazz band, no less. A perfect way to end their honeymoon, sitting outside under the stars, listening to jazz. It would be Dan's last concert.

December 24, 2008

Evening

Dear Ones,

I am breathing deeply on this sacred night, at this sacred time in my life. I am not going to church this evening, but am sitting here in what we call the "piano room" in front of the Christmas tree, just decorated.

I am listening to music that has special meaning to me, connecting me to my sister Anne, who passed away in 2003. The CD is Lauridsen's Lux Aeterna (Light Eternal).

Dan and Natalie had the best time in St. John, U.S. Virgin Islands! Dan likes to talk about moving there. There were spells when he didn't feel very well, but for the most part, he was truly able to soak up the warmth, the sunshine, the tropical beauty. Every day we went to a different beach, and about halfway through the trip Dan commented that he was feeling better than he'd felt in a long time. He swam, he snorkeled, and he and Natalie ate out at some colorful restaurants. I am very grateful that we were able to pull off this trip, with help from many of you. As soon as we got back I put together a photo album for them of about 200 photos. And tomorrow I will give them a framed piece that includes a map of St. John along with photos of them. Many thanks to Heidi at Ben Franklin, who helped put this together so beautifully and so quickly.

As soon as we got back from St. John, Dan started a new clinical trial in Boston. Unfortunately, it has basically been downhill ever since. He got quite sick from some sort of calcium infusion, and the treatment itself has not been very pleasant, though it is not supposed to have many bad side effects. Anyway, to make a long story short, he is uncomfortable and/or in pain a lot of the time. By pain I mean aches, soreness, nausea, difficulty breathing, difficulty eating, etc., and, of course, the emotional pain. He has great trouble sleeping. He gets about three hours a night, if he's lucky. And my once dear little boy, who could tell you with glee about the wonderful smell of snow, now has a fear of the cold. Somehow the cold makes breathing super-difficult, and he feels like he's dying. He dreads going outside. We are now well set up with oxygen, and that helps (especially at night).

Last night coming home from Boston, he said, "Merry Christmas, it's been nice knowing you all." Later on he said, "Mom, what would you do if you were dying?" Of course I have been thinking about this already, and now that he has given me that opening (probably unintentionally), I plan to write him about how I might feel if I were dying, and what I might want to do.

Traveling with Dan through this cancer journey has given me time to reflect on my life—a life review, if you will. I suspect I am at a time in my life when I would be doing that anyway, further integrating my experiences, boiling down my "ingredients" to become a more potent essence for these later years. But Dan's cancer has probably helped to speed up this process for me. Here are a few things I've noted:

About a month ago or so, I realized that I felt so supported by a loving universe. I felt that if I were down and out, without a job or a penny to my name and alone (as I was as a little girl at an English boarding school at age 10), I would really be all right. I have such an amazing family of friends (not to mention my dear Gregg and son Andy) that I know I would be well taken care of. This realization quite took my breath away. For one thing, although I'm quite a decent sort of person, I am by no means in any way amazing or saintly. (Now Natalie, that's another story!) That I could receive such a wealth of what I can only call "unconditional love"—well, I thought that's what the phrase "the grace of God" must mean.

In July 2005, when this strange dog (whom we later named Buddy) showed up at the door of our screened-in porch, I just marveled at his attitude. He was so happy, so joyful, not the least bit afraid. Why wasn't he worried about where his next meal was going to come from? Where was his family? Why did he trust and love me immediately without knowing what kind of person I was? Where were his abandonment issues??!

When I discovered that the name we'd given him came from "Bud," and that its origin meant "herald or messenger," I decided it was indeed quite some miracle that had sent him to us, and that his message was love and joy. He became my role model, how to be love and joy in the world, even at times when you might not know where and when your next meal would be coming from. He continues to be a great teacher for me, as well as for Gregg. Talk about faith and trust!

Here is another thing I remembered the other day. I was in a workshop at the Unitarian Church when Dan was first diagnosed. The program was called "Living by Heart," part of which was to spend time with poetry, learning poems by heart so that you would have them inside you, to nourish and guide your spirit, to deepen your "being-ness." I did not complete the program, but the other day I recalled the only poem I'd memorized (and then later, forgot). I'm sure I partially chose it because it was short and would be easier to memorize. I will include it here for you. It is "The Avowal," by Denise Levertov.

> As swimmers dare
> to lie face to the sky
> and water bears them,
> as hawks rest upon air
> and air sustains them,
> so would I learn to attain
> free fall, and float

into Creator Spirit's deep embrace,
knowing no effort earns
that all-surrounding grace.

*Maybe part of my soul's growth has been to learn to recognize,
to surrender to, and give deep thanks for that all-surrounding
grace.*

I have been reading a book called Courageous Souls: Do We
Plan Our Life Challenges Before Birth? *by Robert Schwartz. The
ideas in this book do not seem "far-out" to me at all, probably
because of my dear sister Anne, who introduced me to "out-there"
ideas at an early age. I find it intriguing to think that our souls
may plan much of what happens to us before birth. And that it's
all about our growth—healing ourselves and the world. I like that
these beliefs help one be less judgmental of oneself and others.
What makes no sense on a human, physical level can be a perfect
plan from the non-physical, soul-level perspective. I guess what I
find comforting is that there could be meaning to the pain, to the
challenges that come our way.*

*It is very hard to bear what is happening to Dan; it is some-
what easier to bear if I can believe that some good is happening,
even if I don't know what that is. Sometimes thoughts like these
flit through my head: What if Dan is working towards being
an amazing healer or teacher in his next life and has chosen
(pre-birth) to experience this most difficult of cancers? What if
he agreed to this challenge on the condition that his true love,
Natalie, would be by his side (and she agreed—pre-birth—to do
this for him)? And I, too, agreed to have a beloved son die of cancer? Could it be that Dan's suffering is somehow not only helping
his own soul's growth but many others as well? Is he giving us
opportunities to express our love, to more deeply appreciate the
gift of life? I will never know.*

I think this way because I just refuse to believe that a young man who is so kind and so gentle a soul could die from some random, meaningless freak of nature such as a rare form of cancer. I think, deep down, I believe in my heart that the mystery we call God, spirit, is a hundred percent Love.

In this extraordinary time of great sorrow, I am so blessed by your love.

BEST WISHES FOR 2009—
Susan/Susie/Sue

P.S. I forgot to mention that Dan recently developed an allergic reaction to the pills on the clinical trial. He has a severe rash (itchy) and was told to stop taking the pills. He will probably not be able to continue on this trial. I don't know what the next step will be.

P.P.S. It's now Christmas Day. Some good news. Dan had his best night's sleep in many days. Thank you, Santa.

P.P.P.S. More good news! Dan is feeling better, maybe because of being off the clinical trial drug. We spent a joyous Christmas evening at their apartment with Natalie's parents—opening presents and enjoying a meal (sumptuous) that Gregg had cooked at home. A very special December 25. Dan even played the piano into the wee hours of the morning.

I WANTED TO TELL some things to Dan before he died. But it was so hard. I wrote him a letter, and even then I could not bring myself to read it to him. I ended up giving it to Natalie and asking her to please read it to him.

I remember going into the nearby bathroom just off their bedroom upstairs in the little apartment they shared in Middlebury. I sat on the edge of the tub and could hear her sweet voice reading.

It was dark outside and quiet and beautiful, the deep of winter. I sobbed while Natalie read the goodbye I could not say.

December 2008

Dear Dan,

I hope it won't freak you out, my writing you a letter. But if you were to die of cancer, or something else, before I die, I would be very sad if I had not written to tell you a few things.

I am so very, very sorry for what you've had to go through these past few years. Granted, there has also been great joy! But too much pain and suffering for one so young and so dear as yourself. As I have often said to you, I would so gladly have changed places with you, for I feel I have had a full and rich and rewarding life. You seem far too young to be leaving this world, though I must say you've managed to pack quite a lot of wonderful experiences into your 26 years. And time really is all relative, isn't it?

Mostly, I want you to know how much you are loved. You were such a dear little baby from the very beginning, and one of your most endearing qualities is that you really have not changed all that much! O.K., sure you've matured and all that, but your "Danny" essence shines through brightly in the mature man you have become. Thomas once described you as "humble," and at the time, I thought it was a bit of an odd adjective to use for you. But since then, I've come to see that it is very apt. You are humble! In that you never crave the limelight or seek attention, you are remarkably without pretense, and you have no idea of the deep ways you have positively affected so many people.

Some things I love about you are: your kindness, your intellect and curiosity, your willingness to forgive and see the best in people (you never seemed to mind that I wasn't a "perfect" Mom), your love of Arthur, your joy of music, your naturalness and refusal to be anything but your true self, the way you eat food with such delight and abandon, the way you wanted to look after me and Dad in our old age ("Mom, I'm never putting you in a nursing home," you said), your determination to accomplish whatever goals you set for yourself, your playful spirit and enjoyment of the simple things in life, your quirky drawings, your big heart, and your funny sense of humor. The list could just go on and on and on...

Now—about this dying thing. If you die before me, I want you to know that although I will miss you terribly, you will still be a very real presence in my life. I will not see you, but I will think of you every day and I will often feel you there...I will probably even have conversations with you. I wish you could think of some way to give me a sign, so that I know it's you, and that you are there. You will at times be close by, I feel sure, just behind the veil, as they say.

I hope you will not be afraid. When the time comes that I am dying, even though I've read quite a bit about dying, I'm sure I will still be a bit afraid. It's natural, the fear of the unknown. But I am hoping that you are not afraid, and that is what I hope for myself, too. From what I've read, when we die we return to a place of great love, peace, and deep serenity. Some people who have near-death experiences have a hard time coming back into their body here on earth, because what they've glimpsed is so wonderful beyond description.

And I know you will have much help crossing over...not only from those you know (for sure, Aunt Anne, Granny, etc.), but also from many angelic beings, some of whom have been looking after you for your whole life. And when I die, I do hope you will be there for me—it will be a joy to meet up with you again.

From readings I have learned that we are not our bodies, nor even our personalities, though those are parts of who we are. We

*are eternal souls, and that is the part of us that never, never dies.
I believe that most of us live many, many lives—with each life
we learn new things. And most of the closest people in our life
we have actually been with before, in past lives (and will be with
again, in a future life).*

*I love you so much Dan, and I thank you for being my son in
this lifetime. You are a wonderful human being, a radiant soul,
and a true blessing for our family.*

Love you forever,
Mom

*P.S. And thank you for the gift of Natalie. We will treasure her
always.*

THE FOLLOWING IS AN excerpt from a letter Dan wrote to
Natalie on December 24, 2008, two weeks before he died. He
was recalling the first time they met, when a mutual friend, Gale,
introduced them at the Co-op, where Dan was working in the
produce department and Gale and Natalie were shopping. Gale
had gone to high school with Dan, and she had shared a suite
with Natalie at Middlebury College.

YOU HAD ME AT _____!

Some cheesy movies say, "You had me at hello," but you actually had me way before hello. I think it was a deep and kind glance that cut background sound like noise cancellation headphones. Gale's mouth was moving, but I don't remember any sound coming out. Something about going to New York City drowned out by being entranced by you. Of course I needed to come back to reality in order to catch your name and that you were Gale's friend and old sweetmate. There were those important details to recall while also focusing on my job of stickering tomatoes and sprinkling arugula. But beyond all the tidbits of information swimming around the room, I knew from that glance that you had me before any sounds became words became sentences. You had me long before hello!!

IN 49.6 YEARS

We can make a toast on our 50th anniversary. I'll put butter and sugar and cinnamon on the toast and we can eat it like our wedding cake, shoveling the sweet bread into each others mouthes. It will truely be the best thing since sliced bread. Then we'll play a duet for our family and celebrate all the love we feel for each other. You'll be 75 and the memory of me an even odd 75. Even in Unity, odd numerically. And that Cinnamon Sugar Toast will be perfectly prepared and so right for such a special event.

Cut toast this way so the heart remains. Eat scraps and then savor the center.

Dan continued on clinical trials pretty much up until the end. In theory that made him ineligible for hospice services. An older person would most likely not have opted for the clinical trials. But Dan was young. He had not lived long enough to make as large a contribution to this world as he might have wished for. Although we did not talk about it, I always thought participating in a clinical trial was one way for Dan to feel he was helping to make a difference, that even if he did not survive, perhaps someone down the road would, thanks to his participation.

But in early January, when he was scheduled to return once more to Dana Farber, he said no. He just couldn't do it. He was having such difficulty breathing. His Middlebury doctor ordered another chest X-ray at Porter Hospital. Dan had not been downstairs for about a week, and it took a long time for him to get down. He sat at the top of the stairs and bumped his way down on his butt, one step at a time, ever so slowly, resting for long periods between steps. The wait at the hospital was interminably long. I remember sitting there next to someone I knew only slightly. I felt between two worlds. Part of me wanted to say to her, "I am here with my son Dan, who is getting a chest X-ray. He is dying of cancer and you probably won't see him again." But I kept quiet.

When Dan went to have blood drawn, the tech told him that her sister had died recently of cancer. Her sister loved to dance, especially Latin American dances. Dan told her when he got to heaven, he would dance the salsa with her sister! There was also a doctor who popped in to say hello. Dan had given his son saxophone lessons. Each encounter, each moment, felt precious. We knew time was running out.

After the hospital visit, we drove to Rubright's, the local donut and bagel shop. I ran in while everyone else stayed in the car. Again, everything was highlighted, etched in our memories because we knew the end was near. We knew this was likely a last tour through town. I was tempted to drive out to our house so Dan could see, one last time, the home where he grew up. But Dan was exhausted, and I think he was also afraid he might need to use a bathroom. So we headed back to his apartment. It turned out to be his last outing, his last donut.

A FEW DAYS LATER, Dr. Armstrong called with the X-ray results. He was surprised Dan could still be alive with his chest so completely full of cancer. It's true Dan's breathing was labored. He could not lie back at all. At night, we stacked pillows and folded blankets in front of him that he then tried to lean over. He could doze off for short periods. The home health nurse came regularly and helped monitor his medication, which seemed quite minimal.

I was impressed that Dan had the wherewithal to be totally in charge. He seemed to know exactly what he was taking and when to take it. But he suffered. This really surprised me, because I thought there were medications now that relieved suffering at the end of life. Maybe, by his own choice, Dan wasn't taking all the pain medication he could have. I don't know. I just know he suffered, and it was especially difficult for him to be unable to lie back against the pillows on his bed. It was wearing him down, and also wearing down those of us who slept in the queen bed next to his hospital bed.

Meanwhile, Dan continued to get up to use the bathroom. He also continued to give music lessons to Natalie. One time he was in the bathroom for what seemed like an hour. Natalie had her music stand set up in the little hallway outside, and was playing flute as Dan called out advice through the door. He said, "I have to teach her everything I know!"

Friends visited Dan during the last weeks of December. Andy came just before Christmas. Natalie's parents were there from

Christmas through New Year's Day. One friend, the brother of Dan's best man, used to come over quite regularly to play music, he on bass guitar and Dan on piano. But now the circle was drawing closer. It was mostly Natalie, Gregg, and me by Dan's side, with visits from the home health nurse. Nat and I slept in the bed next to Dan's hospital bed. Gregg went home to our house at night.

Dan would often do crossword puzzles with Gregg and Sudoku on his own into the wee hours. He listened to music on the CD player. Somehow I heard that Dave Brubeck was on a new CD that Yo-Yo Ma had just put out. I got it at The Vermont Book Shop, where I worked. It is called *Yo-Yo Ma and Friends: Songs of Joy and Peace*. It became one of Dan's favorites, and I still cry when I hear James Taylor singing "Here Comes the Sun."

Jack Johnson's *Curious George* was another CD we listened to over and over again, as well as many others. For Christmas Dan had received a boxed set of DVDs containing the complete episodes of the children's television series *Arthur*. I once asked Dan what he liked so much about that show (he'd watched it right through college). He said he liked it because it was kind. On Wednesday, the day before he died, he had one disc left to view. He really didn't feel well enough to watch it, but he listened to it on the computer, his body bent over the stack of pillows in front of him.

Three days before he died, Dan dictated a letter to Dave Brubeck. He wanted to send him a copy of the CD he'd made. A few of the songs on it were ones Dan had composed, a few were by jazz artists he admired, but most were Brubeck songs. Before I mailed the CD and letter, I copied down Dan's words, knowing everything connected to Dan was precious, to be saved and treasured.

I spent quite a few nights sleeping at the apartment with Dan and Nat. But on January 7, I was really craving a good night's sleep. Gregg agreed to sleep at the apartment while I spent the night at home in nearby Weybridge. The roads were slippery driving there, and not long after I arrived, I got a call from Gregg, who said Dan had asked him to call me. Dan wanted to be sure I'd made it home safely.

I remember sleeping pretty well that night, and when I awoke I was in no hurry to rush back to the apartment. But I got a call from Gregg. Something had changed drastically in Dan's demeanor, and I needed to get there right away.

W HEN DAN DIED, it was shocking. We knew it was coming soon. In fact, just the week before, I had said to someone in the Co-op that there was something worse than dying, and that was not dying—because Dan was so clearly suffering. It was painful to watch. Yet when he died, it was absolutely shocking. He had been here just a moment ago, and now he suddenly was not.

OBITUARY, *ADDISON COUNTY INDEPENDENT*

Daniel Humphrey, 26, Middlebury/Weybridge

Daniel Winn Humphrey, 26, died Thursday, Jan. 8, 2009, surrounded by loved ones.

Dan was born Nov. 26, 1982, in Middlebury, the son of Susan and Gregg Humphrey. He attended Weybridge Elementary School and Middlebury Union High School and graduated from Willamette University in Oregon.

Dan worked for many winters as a snowboard instructor at the Middlebury College Snow Bowl; he also worked at the Middlebury Natural Foods Co-op and Weybridge Elementary School. He also taught piano and saxophone to students locally.

About two years ago Dan developed a rare form of cancer. He tried so hard to stay alive and to relish this gift of life. In July, he married his true love, Natalie Guarin, and in December they went on their honeymoon to St. John.

Dan loved the simple things in life, and he especially loved music. He will be remembered for his indomitable spirit, for being a kind, gentle, and caring man who loved to bike, snowboard, and play music.

He is survived by his wife, Natalie, his parents, Susan and Gregg, his brother, Andy, his sister-in-law, Megan, his nephew, Drew, and his niece, Phoebe, as well as many other dear friends and relatives.

We thank the community for their extraordinary support.

Dan, you opened wide our hearts. A memorial celebration will be held at a later date.

In lieu of flowers, a special music fund will be established in Dan's honor.

January 2009

Dear Friends,

As most of you know by now, our dear Dan passed away on January 8. He suffered quite a bit that last week, but we think perhaps, we hope at least, that at the very end (the very beginning?), there was a letting go of the pain and suffering, a peace at last.

There is so much I could write you. Once again, in the middle of all this disbelief, pain, sadness, anger, grief...there have also been moments of beauty, yes—joy, appreciation, comfort, connection...LOVE.

I am learning that there are so many different feelings to crying. A very hard one is the crying over the what-might-have-been. You see, we not only lost Dan, but we lost a future that we had imagined, without even realizing we'd imagined it. Luckily, I don't seem to go "there" too often. My favorite crying, I've decided, is the one where I'm simply overcome with love for Dan. This, too, is a hard one, but it also feels therapeutic and I feel so close to Dan at these times, and so appreciative of his special, unique personality and how lucky we were to have him in our family.

On the day of Dan's cremation, I read the children's book Tenzin's Deer *out loud to Natalie. The next morning deer came to visit! It truly did feel like Dan was trying to send us a message. I felt so honored by their presence and was really comforted and strengthened by their visit. A few days later I went to check out their path and found that they'd left a mark on the hill, an infinity symbol—more or less. Although it could be the number 8, we think it is most likely the infinity symbol. I know when I first spotted it, my immediate thought was, "Of course, Dan's soul is forever, and, more importantly, Love is forever."*

I realized recently that over the past many months, Dan and I have been doing some sort of "work." It's been a dance, making it up as we go, with very few words. It requires listening to our hearts and to each other's heart. And this work continues. I feel Dan's presence, I feel his inspiration. I bow to him, with a certain degree of surprise that my little Dan, my Danny, my Dan-the-Man, kind, gentle, quirky sense of humor, unassuming, should, in fact, turn out to be a "great one," and a teacher to many.

The outpouring of love and sharing of Dan stories nurtures and sustains us. I have warned Natalie that she may need to tell me to "back off" now and then, because I feel very protective of her. And she is quite bereft. She and Dan shared, and continue to share, a most profound and quite extraordinary love that I have surely been privileged to witness. Her loss is particularly unimaginable. I believe that in some strange way this love of Dan and Nat's has actually gone out into the world, to touch many, many others.

Gregg doesn't write letters the way I do, but he joins me from his heart in saying, "Thank you for all."

Susan, Susie, Sue

P.S. Please keep sending your prayers and good thoughts our way, especially to Natalie.

P.P.S. When I looked up the meaning of "deer," I learned that the ancient Japanese believed them to be messengers of the gods, and that in many cultures, they symbolize gentleness, sensitivity, innocence, and immortality. Here is a poem by Thich Nhat Hanh that recently crossed my path.

No Coming, No Going

This body is not me, I am not caught in this body.
I am life without boundaries. I have never been born,
    and I shall never die.
Look at the ocean and the sky filled with stars,
manifestations of my wondrous true mind.
Since before time, I have been free.
Birth and death are only doors through which we
    pass, sacred thresholds on our journey.
Birth and death are just a game of hide and seek.
So laugh with me,
hold my hand,
let us say goodbye,
say goodbye, to meet again soon.
We meet today.
We will meet again tomorrow.
We will meet at the source at every moment.
We meet each other in all forms of life.

BECAUSE I WAS not there, I asked Gregg to write down his memories of Dan's last night. He had told me briefly about it, but I wanted it in writing. It wasn't until five months after Dan's death, during a trip to Maine that June, that Gregg finally felt ready to do it.

His written piece did not include a few important details he had told me. For example, he said that at one point Dan was counting, "One, two, three, four," and then he said, "I can't count any higher." He also said that Dan had had a nightmare about a fire and burning in the fire. When Gregg roused him, he said, "I'm not supposed to be here; I'm dead." He also repeated over and over, "Hugs from Gregg, help from Natalie," or perhaps it was the reverse.

From Gregg in Maine

Susie and Natalie,

I jotted this off today as best I could. It wasn't easy. Consider it a first draft. Natalie, I know it's your birthday tomorrow, sweet 26 on 6-6, and I hope I can talk to you on the day. I can't wait to see you and to cook a belated birthday feast for you when you arrive in Maine.

Love to all,
Gregg

Just in case either of you cannot open the attachment, here it is:

I remember the alarm going off sometime around 12:30 a.m. It was my time to be upstairs with Dan and to let Natalie try to get some sleep. I lay on the double bed upstairs and listened while Dan tried to breathe, hoping that he would be able to doze off for a while. I did not once feel then that he would soon choose to die.

I drifted off and was jolted awake by Dan yelling, "You assholes, you assholes, you assholes!" I went over to him and tried to talk to him but he was very agitated and in almost a dream-like state, not quite talking in his sleep because he was able to tell me a little about what was going on when I asked him who he was talking about. "The doctors! They knew all the time. They knew!" But it wasn't like we had a regular conversation about this. Far from it. He was drifting off and on from his sleep-like state, and now he was quiet again. I put on a CD, the first one I put my hands on. I sat next to Dan, either on the wheelchair or the porta-potty. I rubbed his back. I probably told him his "dream was over," but it really wasn't a dream at all but a venting that had gone on for several minutes.

As soon as he heard the music he told me that it was the "Goldberg Variations." He wanted me to know that Bach wrote these tunes explicitly for his students, to make it hard on them, and to force them to practice all of the skills they needed to be good at playing. This conversation was a real one. He was up. It was somewhere around 2–3 a.m. He wanted to pee, and remarkably, he was able to get to the porta-potty and to pee. I still did not once think about him dying yet.

I remember the CD ending, and then I put on the Curious George CD. *I may have nodded off again after he got back in his bed. But sometime later in the night/early morning, I went downstairs and brought him some tropical fruit mix. He ate it, which surprised me. He told me it was good. We talked about what was in it and how much we both like mangoes and such. It was so difficult to hear him laboring with his breathing. It seemed especially hard for him, and I remembered how Dr. Armstrong had told us that there was very little space left in his lungs. I'm not sure exactly when Natalie reappeared, but it may have coincided with my next trip downstairs for some more food. He wanted waffles with maple syrup, and that's what I brought him. He ate it all and said it tasted good. I think he especially liked licking all the maple syrup. It was surprising to see him actually eat, since he had only been picking at things for days.*

We both were in the room with Dan now. I remember asking him if he needed any of his meds, especially the painkillers. He told us no. I think I remember him saying that he was not in any pain. At some point I was standing at the foot of the bed and Natalie was in front of Dan. We both noticed that his eyes did not seem to be focusing well. Natalie put up a finger and told Dan to

*follow it as she moved her finger slowly back and forth in front
of his eyes. He tried hard to move his eyes but they still seemed
glazed and drooping. This was unusual, and Natalie said, "Dan,
do you know who this is?" He then gave her a look that was pure
Dan. It was filled with ironic humor as he kind of rolled his eyes
up, as if to say to her "...duh, of course I know who you are." I
moved to his side, and it was then that I saw Dan reach his head
up and kiss Natalie. Perhaps he put his hand up to hold her to his
lips, but I'm not sure about this. This seemed an incredibly long
kiss which, looking back, and now knowing that it was a kiss for
eternity, may have been the actual moment that I knew he was
truly dying. He was in complete control and had been, of course,
for hours.*

*We called Susie. We did what we could to talk to him and be
with him until she arrived, and the home health nurse arrived,
and we got Andy on the phone, and I put his own CD on the
player, and then, calmly, he died.*

I WAS USUALLY DOING some sort of handwork while Dan was
undergoing treatments. I remember working on a pink knitted
vest with white sheep across the front while he received chemo at
the hospital in Burlington. Carrying the yarn over for the sheep
pattern was difficult, and I had to rip it out occasionally when
the stitches were too tight. This vest was for my granddaughter
Phoebe, who must have been almost three at the time. Handwork,
such as knitting or needlepoint, is very calming and grounding,
perfect for keeping vigil. I've never had rosary beads, but I wonder if the repetitive rubbing of prayer beads would be a similar
experience to doing my handwork, because I was always knitting
my prayers into the work.

I knit a shawl for Natalie during the last months of Dan's life.
I had hoped to finish it by Christmas, but it took a little longer. I

finished it about a week or so after Dan died. Here is an odd thing. Preparing to wrap the finished shawl, I laid it out on the bed. The pattern of the stitches was such that the design always appeared to run across and down. But now I saw that on the right side of the shawl, at the part I had last finished, if you looked closely enough you could see that the pattern ran upwards instead. This error must have occurred close to the time Dan died. It certainly did not affect the overall integrity of the shawl, so I did not redo it. In fact, I liked that this "mistake" reflected what was really going on.

Looking back, I appreciate that we didn't know what we were doing with this dying thing. There is something to be said for being brought up in a faith where the dying rituals are laid out for one to follow. One is so devastated and in shock when a loved one dies; the brain is likely to work at half-mast. How comforting to simply slip into prescribed and revered rituals passed down from generation to generation. I imagine one could practically go on autopilot as one moved through the sacred rites, honoring and disposing of the body of the loved one.

But that was not our situation. When I started at Middlebury College in January 1971, the first class I took was a drama course on improvisation. It was probably my favorite course of my whole college experience. So alive! What we did after Dan died was in the same vein; it was improvisational. I think, because of his love for jazz, Dan would have appreciated that. It forced us to be totally in the moment, present for each decision. We had no road map, we had to feel our feelings; and from this deeply felt place, we made decisions about the next step.

Soon after Dan died, I remember going into a little side room off the hallway, where the washer and dryer were housed. From there I made some tearful phone calls. Not long afterwards, one of Dan's close friends arrived, and I believe he and Gregg might have cleaned Dan up a bit, changing some of his clothes, washing his face. This is all a bit of a blur now. At some point, Natalie's friend took her away to her home in nearby Cornwall.

It was a Thursday, and throughout the day, as news of Dan's death spread through town, people stopped by to visit. We didn't plan this, but it seemed a most appropriate impromptu "wake." We set several chairs near Dan's bed so people could go upstairs and sit with him for a few moments. I love that we were not hiding Dan away, nor our sorrow. We had a candle burning near Dan's bed, and the small apartment felt warm and welcoming, and peaceful, too. Because the apartment was right in town, we had a steady stream of visitors off and on throughout the day.

The day before, a social worker from Addison County Home Health and Hospice had talked to Gregg about possible funeral and cremation services. She had given him a few names and numbers he might call. Not long after Dan died, Gregg made some phone calls. He really liked the sound of a fellow named Tom who ran a cremation service in southern Vermont called Eternal Blessings. Tom suggested he come to the apartment the next day, Friday. I was glad Dan's body was not immediately removed after he died. It not only allowed people to stop by to see him one last time, it also gave us time to be with Dan's body and to ease into this new strange place we were in. As strange as it may sound, I especially appreciated being able to sleep that night in the bed next to Dan's bed. It was somehow comforting to wake in the night and to be able to see him resting peacefully nearby.

The next day, Gregg's older brother, Mike, arrived, along with a friend of mine. Tom from Eternal Blessings showed up, and I liked him immediately. His jeans might have had a hole in the knee, and he was wearing a little ski cap very much like the one Dan used to wear. He made himself right at home, sitting for a long time with Gregg at the kitchen table and telling some pretty good stories. He was compassionate and down to earth; best of all, he was in no hurry whatsoever. He suggested we might want to clip a little bit of Dan's hair for a keepsake. He also suggested that we could write Dan a note and stick it in his pocket. I remember Nat doing this.

Finally, it just seemed time.

We stood around Dan and said our goodbyes. We put one of Dan's favorite knitted caps on his head; it was cold and snowy outside. Gregg, Tom, and Uncle Mike helped carry Dan out on a stretcher to the big black SUV that Tom had arrived in. Tom offered to have us follow in our car. I thought about it, but somehow did not feel I needed to go. I totally trusted that Dan was now in Tom's good care. We watched as the black van slowly backed out of the driveway, taking Dan's body to the crematorium.

I DON'T KNOW WHAT Gregg or I will do when one of us dies, but I suspect if a gathering is held, it will be small and private. But with Dan we felt called to do something on a much larger scale. So many in our community knew about Dan's cancer, had been rooting for him, and were deeply moved by his humble yet valiant efforts to live fully, right up to the end. I felt like I had some community role to fulfill, an ambassador of sorts. I was called to invite friends and strangers alike into this sacred honoring of our son's life. We decided not to have a service immediately after his death but wait until May, when we would hold it at Middlebury College's Mead Chapel, a space large enough to contain the many we anticipated would want to attend.

But we did need to do something before then, especially for Natalie. So about a week after his cremation, some friends of Natalie's, some friends of mine, and some co-workers of Dan's gathered in the office of a bodyworker in town, a woman who had worked generously and compassionately with Dan at the end of his life.

I brought red yarn. (When I looked for some yarn in an old container, I found the yarn and the start of a scarf Dan had been knitting when he was little, and I was teaching him to knit.) We passed the ball of yarn and wrapped it around our wrists as each person spoke and shared stories. We laughed and we cried. When the ball had made its way around the entire circle, we cut the yarn between us so that each person had a length with which to make a small braided bracelet, a keepsake of our time together, sharing our stories of Dan.

BEFORE MAILING IT, I wrote down the words to the letter Dan had dictated for Dave Brubeck, to be sent with a copy of Dan's CD. I must have included a short note of my own. Many weeks later I received a letter back from Dave Brubeck. He had written it on paper from a yellow legal pad, just like my father used to write his letters on.

Dear Dave,

Thanks for taking "Time out" of your busy schedule to chat last June in Burlington. You truly have inspired me as a pianist as well as a person. I'll do my very best to warm up the band in heaven so that the celebration will be ready for you and Iola. In the meantime, keep going with your phenomenal work.

Love,
Dan

P.S. I have included some of my own music and renditions of some of your compositions, as well as those of other respected musicians.

Dear Susan,

I have just received your letter and the letter that Dan dictated to Natalie. I immediately put "ONCE" on my player and have admired all the music and piano playing and thought that went into producing this album. What an inspiration it is to me to hear Dan today knowing it will inspire me the rest of my life. How kind he is being to all of us that knew him to leave our faith intact because his faith was so strong. He is keeping a corner in heaven for us so we can all join together in a great celebration and of course a promised two-piano concert.

Love from,
Dave and Iola
Feb. 4, 2009
Sanibel Island, FL

IN MY DATE BOOK, for February 23, 2009, I have written "The 1st day of no cards-Dan." The very next day I have written "Cards Dan again."

For well over a month we received sympathy cards every day. Going down to the mailbox became my favorite daily ritual. I cannot begin to express how much those cards meant to me. And I loved them all. The "old" me liked cards but not what I called "Hallmark-y" cards—the ones with trite or sappy messages. But the me during this period loved them all! I cried over each and every one of them. And the crying felt not so much like sadness, but more like overwhelming love. Love for Dan, but also love for anyone who remembered Dan and mentioned his name.

Deep mid-winter seemed the perfect time to die. I don't know why that would be so, but the cold white snow, the quiet landscape, keeping cozy by the wood stove—it just felt right. And I wanted time to stand still. When Dan first died, shocking as it was, we were held in a bubble of love, an outpouring of compassion and kindness from so many.

But time is ever moving on.

I remember being somewhat appalled when I realized that people were getting on with their lives. They had not forgotten Dan, but other commitments and interests were now taking precedence. And even the seasons were being fickle; how dare winter slowly give way to spring?! It seemed so unfair, a betrayal. How could everything move on without Dan?

CRAWLSPACES

2009–2011

…a descent to a state of death in life.

—Miriam Greenspan, *Healing Through the Dark Emotions*

March 27, 2009

Dear Friends,

I've thought of you all so often but wanted to wait to write you until I could be certain of the date, time, and place for Dan's Celebration of Life service.

The celebration for Dan will be May 16 (Saturday) at 2 p.m. at Mead Chapel (Middlebury College). It is a large space—all are welcome—and the only thing that I can tell you for sure is that there will be music!!

How are we? I really can only speak for myself, though, in my opinion, I would say that we are all doing well, grieving each in our own way, with ups and downs. For me, at times I am still quite overcome with the enormity of this loss. I know that this is a life-transforming experience, though I do not yet know what this means for the future. I live day by day. And I keep coming back to LOVE. It has been there, a guiding force, all along, and I continue to have faith in its power and steadfastness. Love is eternal. I am so grateful to have felt the presence of Love throughout Dan's cancer journey. I am trusting that it will continue to guide us, to bless us, to comfort us, to inspire us in the days, the months, the years ahead.

For me, Dan has pretty much become synonymous with love. And sometimes I think that what Dan has gone and done, perhaps unintentionally, is broken open my heart (and other hearts) so that I can truly know love at a deeper level. I am hoping this sacred sorrow, as I call it, will help me to be a more loving person in the world. I have definitely, already, had moments where I've been quite overcome with love for others. I don't know if this is just a phase in the grieving process, or if it will last. We'll see.

Almost every day, at least quite often, I could say, I am in awe and wonder at how life is unfolding. Little synchronicities, "A-ha"

77

moments, glimpses into patterns, and how one thing leads to another, interconnections. Again, a feeling that there is a quite beautiful, one could almost say perfect, pattern to this mystery we call Life. This, too, sustains me on an almost daily basis.

It is possible I will create something—a book? who knows—in Dan's honor. A few days ago a phrase popped into my head: "What am I going to do with all this Love?" Hopefully, the love that Dan has awakened in me can come out in some creative way, not only to help others, but also to honor my dear Dan. I do have the dearest grandchildren (no, I'm not exaggerating!), and I am so grateful for that most obvious of places toward which to direct my love. But who knows? Dan will be a powerful muse. He already is, and with his help, much is possible. Love is limitless.

I believe I mentioned the deer (practically coming to my doorstep) in my last letter. I had another memorable deer experience the day Natalie (with my help) closed up the apartment and headed home to Millbrook. This was an extremely sad day, saying "Goodbye" to the apartment they had shared, and again, to the life they had hoped to live. I came home broken-hearted, but through my tears, as I turned onto Thompson Hill Road, I could see 12 deer in a nearby field. I have since learned that the deer was Dan's totem animal. I don't know if Dan was trying to communicate with me—but I can tell you how comforted I was by the presence of the deer.

Hope you all can come on May 16! We are also planting a tree (and name plaque) in Dan's honor at the Middlebury College Snow Bowl, where he loved to snowboard and teach snowboarding.

Love to you all!
Susan/Susie/Sue

P.S. <u>More</u> things to tell you—

I bought Natalie a book, Healing After Loss: Daily Meditations for Working Through Grief. *And I bought myself a copy. I love reading one page a day, and knowing that Natalie is also reading the same page. (We do keep in touch on a regular basis.)*

The Dan Humphrey Music Scholarship has been established!! This will allow students from grades 9–12 at MUHS to receive financial help to attend a summer music camp. If you would like to contribute in Dan's honor (truly, the smallest amount is ample) please make a check out to The Dan Humphrey Music Scholarship. Thanks so much!

Here is a poem I wrote shortly after Natalie closed the apartment and moved back home to Millbrook, NY. She had given me some of Dan's clothes, etc., to take back home, and other things to store. I also have some of Dan's phone messages taped on a cassette.

Loving Dan

Please don't try to cheer me up
Let me wallow in my grief a while
Folding a familiar shirt, putting away
The single sock
I hear your voice messages on the phone
Hey, Mom, this is Dan.

Please don't try to cheer me up
These tears are just my love expressed
Why does it take loss to make
Presence so dear—
Will there ever be a day I don't

Remember that you're not here?
Hey, Dan, this is Mom.

I listen to your music playing
Remember your funny ways
I see you in all the same old places
Your look, your glance
Here, but not here, where are you Dan?
Where did you go, Dan?
The deer stand sentinel, kind and strong
Hey, God, this is Dan.

THE FOLLOWING POEM was inspired by Priscilla Baker's personal guided story and imagery exercise at Hospice Volunteer Services. I wrote it in the early morning of April 3, 2009. I woke up with the phrase "we all should have a playroom" in my head, and the rest flowed from there.

A Place to Grieve

We all should have a playroom
A secret space inside,
With paints in little boxes and
Some metal pans beside.
We can slide across the paper
Our fingers deft and quick,
Or dance our hearts out on the floor
Turning, bending, kick.
There are no judges in this room
The colors soft and warm,
Sometimes we sit so quietly

Our feelings need to yearn.
We write, we paint, we move
We wait in stillness, too,
And most of all remember
The one who brought us through.
The one who brought us to this place
Who opened wide our hearts,
The one who left us way too soon
Yet fills us with this grace.

We all should have a playroom
A secret space inside,
A stairway into heaven
Where our loved one does reside.

June 23, 2009
Southwest Harbor, Maine

Dear Friends,

We have been in Maine and return to Vermont tomorrow. Natalie and her family came to stay with us for a few days. It was good to share with them this special place that was dear to Dan's heart. We sprinkled some of Dan's ashes here and there.

I was thinking about this letter-writing business...how natural it was for me to pick up pen and paper when Dan's cancer was first diagnosed. Over time, I have remembered that one of the most difficult times in my life was at age 10 when I was at the English boarding school on the island of Barbados. Letters were the only contact I had with anyone who truly knew and cared about me. Those letters probably kept me sane. You all have thanked me for sharing this cancer journey with you, but I thank you for being there, for receiving so open-heartedly whatever it is I've needed to share. The letter-writing has helped keep me sane and connected, and the channels open.

They say, "Be careful what you wish for".... Did I tell you this already? One day I remembered that whenever I have to make a wish (blowing out candles, throwing a coin in a well, etc.), I almost always make the same wish—to feel more loving. Not to be or feel more loved, but to feel, in myself, more love for the world, for others. Sometimes now, I want to say to the universe, "But I didn't mean like this! I didn't mean I wanted to feel more loving by having my heart broken open!" Sometimes the gifts we are given are confusing. Sometimes it is hard to keep saying every day, "Thank you for everything exactly the way it is right now." Hard... but still, a worthy practice.

Thank you to all who were able to come to Dan's service on May 16. I woke up at about 2 a.m. that morning and lay in bed knowing what an important, a momentous day it would be... and I hoped I would not be a walking zombie by the afternoon. The service was everything we could have hoped for. There was no dress rehearsal; we didn't know what others were going to say or share. But it all just seemed to flow effortlessly.... Many of us could feel Dan there, and he was loving it! He had a big grin, he couldn't believe how awesome the music was, and parts of the service made him laugh out loud. And I feel sure there were others present, as well, from that invisible realm—so many of us could just feel it. We all rose to the occasion, every one of us there, our best selves, to be there for Dan. It was truly a glorious celebration. And for me, I even felt that we created something in Dan's honor that went beyond Dan. The vibration of love in that chapel... surely we gave the universe a most positive boost that day.

The morning after the service we sprinkled some of Dan's ashes around a tree planted in his memory up at the Middlebury College Snow Bowl where Dan loved to snowboard, and where he was an instructor for many years. The tree is a Canaan fir (pro-nounced Ka-nane I believe) and is very similar to a Balsam. The branches are soft and smell good! The tree is in the most beautiful spot—near a running stream and near to where snowboarders gather for their classes. A spot quiet, beautiful in the summer and full of action in the winter. We said a few words of blessing in Dan's honor (I think I may even have read a winter poem Dan once wrote on a Christmas Eve), and we also honored Dan by drinking his favorite Monument Farms chocolate milk and eating his favorite donuts from Rubright's Bakery. (There were always free donuts from Rubright's available in the instructors' room up at the Snow Bowl.)

Thank you, also, to those of you who chose to contribute to the music scholarship in Dan's memory. We received enough contributions to have this scholarship go for at least seven years! Wow! The first scholarship was awarded to a worthy trumpet player in the jazz ensemble at Middlebury Union High School. He is going to a jazz music camp for two weeks. Dan would be so very pleased. The recipient seems to be a fine young man, so appreciative, with lots of music potential.

I love Maine—but it also holds a bit of melancholy, nostalgia, and memories of times gone by for me. This year I can feel that sadness the same as always, but now Dan's passing adds to it. I tear up at unexpected moments. Sometimes I am even surprised at how "big" Dan's not being here on this earth is. I have lost both parents, four brothers and sisters, their spouses, but nothing really compares to this. I will close with the passage I read as we scattered some of Dan's ashes here in Maine.

Love,
Me

Peace, My Heart

Peace, my heart, let the time for
the parting be sweet.
Let it not be a death but completeness.
Let love melt into memory and pain
into songs.
Let the flight through the sky end
in the folding of the wings over the
nest.
Let the last touch of your hands be
gentle like the flower of the night.
Stand still, O Beautiful End, for a
moment, and say your last words in
silence.
I bow to you and hold up my lamp
to light you on your way.

—*Rabindranath Tagore*

*P.S. I hope all is well with you and your loved ones. And again,
many many thanks!*

*P.P.S. Although they are happening less frequently, we continue to
have what we call "Dan moments," things that happen that seem
just slightly out of the ordinary and that remind us of Dan. Often
there is a bit of humor, too. Here is an example of one:*

*One evening in early June when Gregg was in Maine and I
was on my own at home, I was thinking so much about Dan as
I searched through the cupboard looking for tuna fish. I finally
found a package of Bumble Bee brand. Checking out the expira-
tion date, I noticed that it said on the package "Product of Trini-*

*dad and Tobago." I thought that was the weirdest random thing!
I used to live in Tobago (when I went to that English boarding
school on Barbados). I remembered how the first trip Dan and
Nat took together was to Trinidad and Tobago.*

 *Later that night I called Natalie and said, "I think I might have
had another Dan moment." I told her about the tuna fish. She
said, "You know, in Trinidad we stayed with my friend, Annalise.
Dan and I used to laugh at the name of the town. It was called
Tuna Puna!" Was Dan really playing with us? Who knows? But it
gave us a smile—and I wouldn't put it past him.*

HOLDING DAN'S CELEBRATION service at Middlebury College
was a natural choice. Both Gregg and I had gone to Middlebury
and Gregg was currently a professor in Education Studies there.
Laurie Jordan, chaplain of the College, would officiate, with
numerous speakers and musicians offering their gifts. We liked
the idea of celebrating there for so many reasons, not the least
being we needed a large space. We met with Laurie months ahead
of time. She advised us to plan out the service as best we could,
and not to have an open mike where others would be invited to
share their stories of Dan. We could save that for the gathering
after the service. She had had experiences where an open invitation to share had meant a service that went on way too long for
the comfort of most of the guests. Anticipating a large turnout,
we took her suggestion to heart and planned accordingly.

 We were having lunch at our house with the Guarins on that
beautiful Saturday in May when I suddenly realized the time. I
should have been at the chapel about an hour in advance, but
there I was in the entry at 1:45 p.m., with 15 minutes to spare, still
hastily setting up some photographs of Dan taken throughout
his life, placing them on entry tables. So, right from the get-go, it
was a service different from most. Instead of being off-stage and

out of sight—or sitting quietly in our pew, removed from those coming in—I was in the entry greeting the first guests, as though to a party at my home, while quickly finishing the display of photographs.

We had neglected to pin down specific seating arrangements. I ended up in a front pew on the right with Natalie and Andy and his family. Gregg sat across the aisle with his bandmates. The Middlebury High School Jazz Band was set up in front on the right. Just fitting all of those students and their instruments in that small space was a feat unto itself.

The music was out of this world. The jazz band was glorious, playing some of Dan's favorites and ending with Paul Desmond's "Take Five," under the direction of Anne Severy and based on Tito Puente's arrangement. Gregg's band, Snake Mt. Bluegrass, played a moving rendition of "The Battle Hymn of Love" by Tim O'Brien and the ever-joyful "Dancin' with the Angels" by Peter Rowan. Somewhere in the middle of the service, there was even an impromptu interlude where some of Dan's music buddies stepped forward to perform a piece that was not on the program.

Anne Severy, director of the MUHS Band and Jazz Band, had been like a mother to Dan throughout his high school years: a combination of mother, teacher, friend, and mentor. She was his homeroom teacher, and Dan spent most lunchtimes in her classroom, seated on the couch with friends, talking about music and life. After Dan had his leg amputated, she invited him to help out in the classroom now and then, to share his knowledge and love of music with the younger students. "Sev," as the students called her, spoke at length about Dan and the good and often hilarious times they had shared when he was a student at MUHS. One story involved her picking up Dan and a few other students early from their Project Graduation party so they could head up to Burlington to hear Dave Brubeck playing at the Flynn Theater. Sev had us laughing, and crying too.

The service lasted a couple of hours but felt much shorter; time flew by. We were all uplifted by the energy in that room. Each offering in the program seemed so special; it was as though the occasion had brought out the very best in each of us. There were probably over 300 people present, honoring and loving Dan. To this day, friends and acquaintances occasionally tell me that it was one of the most amazing and memorable services they've ever attended. The stars were somehow aligned just right on that day.

A TRIBUTE TO DAN
(I read this at Dan's service)

Dan was such a sweet and cuddly little boy. And he grew up to be a kind and gentle man.

I used to tell people that my children are spaced about four years apart because it took me that long to forget how painful childbirth was! But that is only part of the truth. The other part is that I was so in love with my firstborn, Andy, I just didn't think it would be possible to love another child as much. I was afraid I wouldn't be a good Mom if I didn't love my children equally. But then we threw caution to the wind, and on November 26, 1982, the morning after Thanksgiving Day, Daniel Winn Humphrey was born into this world. And much to my relief and joy, the miracle of falling in love happened all over again.

When Dan was about four years old, we had this conversation about marriage. In those days we called him Danny. He didn't understand why he couldn't marry me when he grew up. I explained how I was already married to Daddy, and that when he grew up, he would fall in love with someone his own age. And 22 years later he did. Her name is Natalie.

I think there were probably some decisions in Dan's life that he was not 100 percent sure of. But the one decision I know he was completely sure of was marrying Natalie. Dan was extremely unlucky to get this rare form of cancer, extraskeletal myxoid chondrosarcoma. But he was also the luckiest man in the world to meet and marry Natalie Guarin. I say you could go a lifetime without experiencing the depth of love those two shared. For me, what a gift it was to be able to witness up close such a love as theirs. Words are simply inadequate.

Sometimes, when I am very sad, it is helpful and comforting to remember that Dan loved his life. He thought he had the best childhood ever! He never seemed to mind that I wasn't the perfect Mom. He loved Christmases in Craftsbury, annual trips to Virginia and Maine, and most of all growing up in Weybridge, Vermont. He loved school, except for maybe seventh grade, and his family and friends. He and Natalie had even talked of maybe one day building a house on our property. They would live next door and look after Gregg and me in our old age.

Dan showed a determined streak at quite a young age. Once his mind was made up, he could not be easily deterred. In kindergarten he announced that he was going to walk the whole 10 kilometers for the Crop Walk. Gregg tried to bribe him out of it halfway through, but there was no stopping Dan. Gregg hitched a ride back, but I had to walk the whole way with Dan.

Dan was also very much his own person. He was kind of a goofy, easy-going kid, and was never overly concerned about what others thought of him. He marched to his own drummer. In kindergarten, and even through much of first grade, during journal time when the other children were practicing inventive spelling and writing cute things that any mother would be proud of, my Dan was drawing intricate mazes instead. I still can't believe his teacher, Miss Carlson, let him do that!

Dan also had a quirky sense of humor—that became apparent early on. When he went for his preschool early-education screening, the first question they asked him was, "What is your name?" Dan gleefully replied, "Lettuce!" He thought he was being so funny, and I thought, "Oh brother, they're going to recommend him for special ed!"

Dan really made the most of the last few years of his life. He took pride in studying and getting into a difficult graduate program at UVM. He worked hard at learning to walk again with a prosthetic leg and was determined he would bike, run, and snowboard again. He married the love of his life, Natalie, and they honeymooned on St. John. He taught music lessons and put together a CD of his own piano playing to give to family and friends. Most of all he loved sharing life with Natalie.

But I also want you to know that Dan suffered. It was not easy losing his leg and experiencing severe phantom pain. And towards the end, everything became so very difficult—eating, sleeping, and even breathing. I am telling you this not to be gruesome, but because it seems quite remarkable to me now, looking back, that Dan somehow managed not to become totally self-absorbed and self-pitying. He really was incredibly courageous, and he always cared about others, right up to the end. The last thing Dan said to me, the night before he died, was to please be careful driving home. He made me promise not to go down the steep hill but to take the longer route home because the road conditions were a bit iffy. And then later that night Gregg called me because he said Dan wanted to be sure I'd made it home safely.

Yes, there has been despair, sadness, and even anguish on this journey. But there has also been laughter, joy, and hope. For Dan and Natalie perfected the art of living in the moment. And the great truth that I learned from the privilege of journeying by their side is that, even in one's darkest hour, there, too, is *love*. Isn't that the miracle? That love is present in each moment, and it is forever.

We do believe that Dan came to be at peace at the end of his life here on earth. The last night Natalie told me she got Dan ready for bed early on. They were trying to do a crossword in a book, but he really couldn't focus. So she made one up. She said to Dan, "It's a three-letter word, and is someone I love very, very much!"

And then he had to give her one. He said, "It's a four-letter word, starts with an 's' and means to take flight." The answer was soar, S-O-A-R.

Dan, my dear Dan, you soared. You truly soared. I don't know why you had to die so young, but in your quiet, unassuming way you somehow became quite extraordinary and touched the lives of many. You taught us so much about appreciating each moment, and about enjoying the simple things. You taught us about living with hope and courage, and—ultimately—with acceptance. You opened us to love, and the world is a better place because you were in it.

We love you, Dan. We miss you, and you will be forever in our hearts. Amen.

I HAVE TWO NOTEBOOKS filled with brief entries, recording things that seem important to me to remember. Most of these entries catalog the many inexplicable coincidences and synchronicities that occurred in the days, weeks, months, and even years after Dan died. Some are fairly astonishing. But I believe that after the death of a loved one, especially a particularly shattering death, *everything* takes on new significance, and one starts to see meaning in the most mundane of happenings.

Immediately after a death, one can still feel the presence of the loved one as though a part of his or her essence is still floating around. You feel very close to what some call the "Other Side." You are attuned to noticing everything: the early morning light casting a cruciform shadow on the window; a book falling off a shelf and opening to the page one needed to read; a song coming on the radio—one you have never heard before—and the feeling that it is playing just for you.

Not long after Dan died I was folding some laundry when I suddenly heard a song playing that I recognized from the *Curious George* CD we had listened to so often. It was playing in the next room and I ran over, half expecting to see Dan there. It was as though he had called to me. It turned out the song was coming from the TV; it was an advertisement for PBS. I had never seen or heard this advertisement before, nor have I since.

Are our loved ones sending us messages? Or are we so shaken by their deaths that we imagine we are being given signs? I don't know and it doesn't really matter. What matters is that all of the inexplicable happenings (I call them "Dan moments") brought me great comfort, an expanded sense of self, and a deeper connection to spirit and to what some call God. For this I am grateful.

ONE DAY I WAS DRIVING in my car with Dan on my mind, as usual, and remembering—reliving, really—the morning Dan died. And for some reason, that brought to mind a favorite picture book that I hadn't thought about in a long while. The book is *Mole and the Baby Bird* by Marjorie Newman, illustrated by Patrick Benson.

In this story, Mole befriends an abandoned baby bird. He looks after the bird until it grows up and one day is ready to fly. But Mole is not ready to lose his friend. He builds a cage to keep Bird from flying away. Bird is very sad, sitting in that cage. Fortunately, wise Granddad Mole comes to visit and helps Mole realize what he needs to do. I especially love the two-page spread that shows Mole at the top of a big hill where Granddad has taken him. Up on the hill, Mole feels the wind trying to lift him. He feels the grandeur and the awesome mystery of this world, and gains the perspective he needs. When he returns home he opens the cage and lets his beloved Bird fly free. Mole is very sad, but he is glad, too.

I don't buy many picture books for myself, but this one particularly spoke to me the day I first read it. It reminded me of when I was little and once cared for an abandoned baby bird. Most of all, it spoke to my heart. It reminded me of all the many goodbyes we as parents are called upon to make as we watch our children grow up and leave home in ever-widening circles. As parents, we do not own our children; our sacred task is to raise them and then to love them so much that we are willing to let them go. This book also brought to mind the ways in which we let go of loved ones at the end of their lives, when their time has come.

I can't say that I ever thought, when I bought this book, that I would be a parent saying a final goodbye to my son. I am certain that possibility never crossed my mind.

In retrospect, I can think of many things I could have perhaps done differently or better towards the end of Dan's life that would have made his journey a little more comfortable. When you are in the middle of the dying process with someone you love, you don't always think very clearly. But I am very proud of one thing: that at the end, we did not try to hold Dan back.

During the last week of Dan's life I noticed that his back reminded me of the body of a bird. Perhaps because the tumors had crowded all the air out of his lungs. I noticed how his shoulder blades protruded sharply out of his back. With his labored breathing, he looked like a delicate bird with bent wings, trying to catch its breath. His rib cage had become a kind of bird cage.

The last morning, when I arrived at Dan's apartment, he appeared to be unconscious but was still breathing. I like to believe he knew I was there. It all happened so quickly. Suddenly, we knew it was Dan's time. We did not confer, but we knew what we were there to do. It was not a time for remorse or crying, that would come later. It was not about our loss, or our pain. It was about being there for Dan, stepping forward in love to help him take flight.

Gregg quickly switched the CD in the player so that it was playing Dan's piano music, the music he himself had recorded. Dear, beautiful, loving Natalie was holding Dan on one side, and I was on the other. I can't remember exactly what I said. I know I blurted out words of encouragement, something about how we loved him and to go towards the light. I think I said that loved ones were there to help him on this journey. What I was really saying, in so many words, was, "Fly, Dan, soar! Your spirit is free at last. We love you, and we will meet again someday."

And then he was gone.

November 2009

Dear Friends,

I thought I was done with these group letters I've been sending... but I feel some of you wondering how we are doing. And there are always more stories to tell!

Any sorrow can be borne if you can turn it into a story.
—Isak Dinesen

Firstly, know that we are managing. Gregg, me, Andy, dear Natalie—we are out in the world living our lives. Some days are better than others. Recently I read in my daily meditation book (Healing After Loss), "Grieving is such a roller-coaster ride." And the affirmation of the day was, "I will not be discouraged by the mood swings of grieving, but realize they are part of the road to health." I know that for some people grief can be completely debilitating; I am grateful we are all managing as well as we are. And I feel sure that our community of friends is one of the reasons for this. Thank you, thank you.

One of the stories to tell you actually happened this past spring. I found a letter I had written to Dan in his senior year of college (2005). Even back then, for some reason I had the good sense to make copies of letters that felt significant. I copied this one before sending it off to Dan. He was having a difficult time completing his senior thesis on Rilke. Although naturally talented in math and sciences, he had decided to be an English major, of all things. That spring of 2005, he was also experiencing some mental/emotional instability that concerned both Gregg and me. He was fragile, and not himself.

Anyway, what I wrote him about, among other things, was that I was remembering a pattern...that this had happened before. I recalled other times when Dan was having trouble and could not complete an assignment. It was almost like a déjà vu. And what I remembered was that in the end, after quite a bit of struggle and angst, it had worked out. In the end there had been joy and a great sense of accomplishment. I wrote to him to reassure him that I felt sure the pattern would prevail, and that in the end, all would be well.

These few times of extreme difficulty for Dan were also very hard on me. Honestly, they felt like life and death situations somehow (real game-changers in the journey of life). Now, looking back, I almost wonder if they were practice challenges in preparation for the big one, Dan living with cancer and dying well.

What was so special about my happening to come across this letter, which I had long forgotten about, was that it was a reminder of the pattern, and in finding the letter, it almost felt like this time Dan was trying to comfort and reassure me—that he had wanted me to find it and to remember that one comes through the struggle to joy on the other side. I remembered the deer that showed up after he died. And being so close to Easter when I found the letter, I couldn't help but see a parallel to the Easter story—the journey through darkness and despair to the joy of resurrection and new life.

One thing I've noticed is that something seems to happen to one's brain in grief, and this seems to change over time. Time has a different feel, and all kinds of memories surface in no particular order. The gift in this may be that one can see things, and make connections, in ways one would not ordinarily do. It's hard to describe, but it feels rich somehow, and creative, too. Almost as though one has been given access to enter places one could not go to before.

I've been curious about my lack of interest in reading books about grief. At some point, I realized I really wanted to experience directly my own grief. I can so easily fall into a comparative mode; I certainly have not wanted to unleash any "shoulds" on myself. It has reminded me of when I taught kindergarten and how, at times, it was important to refrain from directly "teaching," to step back and let the children make their own discoveries and not compare themselves to others or to some narrow expectation. Maybe I've been trying to do the same for myself—to experience my grief directly, not filtered or tempered through the reading of others' experiences.

Yes, I am still taking photos and making them into cards. I am glad that this "practice" of attending to beauty was firmly established long before Dan got cancer. It has helped me in many ways.

The story I've really been wanting to tell you, and sort of leading up to, happened quite recently. (Years ago an acquaintance told me, "There are no coincidences, just 'God-incidences'!") A few weeks ago a chance (ha!) encounter with a friend led to a conversation about Ram Dass and my remembering that I thought I had *some books by him. Two days later, I literally woke up thinking I must look for those books. I found them on a bookshelf I had inherited from my oldest sister, Anne. But the books were not by him after all; he had simply written the introductions. Then, my eye caught the word "death," and I pulled out this slim book next to the others. It is called* The Death of the Prophet, *by Jason Leen. I have no idea where this book came from but am guessing it belonged to Anne. I opened it to some random page in the middle of the book and couldn't believe what I was reading. It was what one might call a transcendent moment. I felt like I was suddenly lifted out of ordinary time and in touch with Large Life, God, Mystery, Source of All, whatever you want to call it. It was as though those very pages, sitting there undisturbed for years, had been waiting for me and for this time, and that the Universe had conspired to lead me to them. Ram Dass was simply a ruse along the way. I have since read the whole book, but it was those pages I first opened to that were the most meaningful, and the ones I was meant to find.*

I don't know if I am very good about putting into words what a profound experience this was for me. It caused me to flash back to the deer coming to the house the day after Dan's cremation—the deer (their hoofprints possibly mixed in with human footprints?) who left the number 8 in the snow, also the infinity sign. It was like dominoes falling into place. The message from the deer in the snow in January, the pattern remembered in the found letter and the Easter story in April, and the pages discovered this month in a random book opening all carried the same message—that death is not the end! Something continues on. Dan's body may have died but some part of Dan (soul) continues on.

These holy moments that I only rarely experience fill me with wonder and gladness, because I remember, at a very deep level of my being, that "the dance of life continues on even though the dancer's steps are silent." I become "swept up" and "soar beyond boundaries of life and death," much like Dan did (quotes from Jason Leen).

Now that I have a computer, I've gone back to look again at the symbolism for the number 8, also known as the infinity sign. It's pretty amazing. At the end of this letter I will include some of it, as well as the pages from the book that I stumbled upon.

Blessed be! Love to all!
Susan/Susie/Sue

P.S. Other news:

Gregg's beloved brother Tom (age 59) died on August 24. He was in poor health, but it was unexpected. Hadley Winn Humphrey (Andy and Megan's third child, a daughter) was born on August 26. Winn is a name from Gregg's side of the family and is Dan's middle name and Tom's too.

Dan's birthday, November 26, falls on Thanksgiving Day this year.

P.P.S. Contributions continue to arrive. Although we had no particular goal in sight, the Dan Humphrey Music Scholarship now has over $8,000 (there's that magic #8 again!). The young trumpeter who received the first DH Music Scholarship and spent two weeks at a summer jazz camp just got the highest score in both district concert and district jazz ensemble!

P.P.P.S. I dreamt of Dan this morning (November 12). He was a little boy, maybe around 3 or 4 years old. We played baseball together and walked and talked. He had his hand in mine; in my dream I could feel it. A sweet, sweet funny little boy. He was happy!

Some things I found on the computer when I looked up the number 8 (there's a lot more if you care to look yourself):

- *Musically, the diatonic scale has seven notes: Do, Re, Mi, Fa, So, La, Ti, but the eighth note is Do again, at a brand new beginning and on a higher level. (Dan is on a higher level!)*
- *Number of perfection, infinity. In mathematics the symbol of infinity is represented by an 8 laid down.*
- *It is the symbol of the New Life, the final resurrection.*
- *8 is a number from Heaven. All creation is built on 7s. 7 is earth's perfection, but 8 is heavenly perfection.*

Here are pages 46 and 47 from The Death of the Prophet, *by Jason Leen. I couldn't believe I opened to these pages:*

> *Ay, and passing far beyond the man-made meaning for that word, you shall realize that the family is much more than a closeness of kin or a gathering out of convenience and circumstance: family is the relation of one loving heart to another.*
>
> *Once that relation is truly understood, the whole of Creation shall be bathed in the very light which has soared from the deepest space to ignite your heart.*
>
> *And thus, Sarah, the whole universe shall be consumed by that flame and naught shall remain save love. This very love surrounds us ere we are born and, likewise, naught save this love truly nourishes our lives.*
>
> *For even as you give birth unto your children, so shall they continue to be born anew unto the universe as each moment is born anew.*
>
> *And in that perpetual rebirth they are forever surrounded by love.*
>
> *Verily, as they came dancing the dance of Life, so shall they*

continue to dance throughout the ages. Ay, for even as another has promised you, your life is without end.

Yet seek not to understand nor control the patterns of your children's dancing, nor become afraid when you can no longer hear the tune to which they step.

Rather would I have you relax your heart in peace, knowing that they dance but to the very music which has moved you— and that their movements have been but altered themselves to better suit the nature of the dancer.

And become not consumed by sadness if your children's dancing should cease to be, for know beyond any doubt that the dance of Life continues on even though the dancer's steps are silent.

If you could but fathom this, you would be swept up in that very movement and soar beyond the boundaries of life and death.

For you are Light, created by Light from the essence of Light: and that which you create is Light.

Even as you give birth and the child moves from within your womb into the air of this world, it is but Light issuing from Light into Light.

March 13, 2010

Dear Friends,

I don't think I made any promises to you out loud, but I think an unspoken promise I made, and perhaps it was just to myself, was that I would try to be as truthful as I could be, in whatever it was I would choose to share with you.

I was intending to write you a little sooner; I could hear some of you wondering how we were doing. But just about the time I thought I would write, I suddenly lost myself. Me, the person who writes you, was not capable of being wholly (holy?) there. So what I would write to you now, if I am to be truthful, is that I still feel a little shaky, but more "me" again, thank God. I would tell you that there is something worse than losing one's child, and that is losing yourself. This happened to me once before, in 1988, I think it was. It was the scariest thing. And though the terror subsided, it took many years. I never did return to who I was.

All through this grieving over Dan, I have been so grateful that even though at times I have been so sad, and certainly in the beginning disoriented, I still felt connected to Love! I don't want to spend much time here telling you about what it feels like to feel disconnected. But I will tell you that it is absolutely the scariest thing. Have you ever felt that way?

There were a series of things that happened and I don't even know which, or if all of them, caused me to suddenly feel so strange. I did have two nights in a row when I didn't sleep—at all! Gregg gave me a good word. He said it's "deranging" not to sleep. And I thought, "That's it! I feel deranged." One thing that is so painful about being in this "lost" space, is that even if love and support is all around you, you are not in a place where you are able to feel and know this. I will tell you that I was so scared I prayed. I prayed to whatever spirit guides I might have out there; I prayed to Dan. I tried to continue with whatever routines seemed "normal" or healthy. Simple tasks. I dusted. I straightened. I walked my dog. I went to work. Over time the world started to right itself again, and I felt more grounded and there.

I have thought about those earthquakes [in Chile]...I even wondered if it was possible that I was somehow feeling them, from this great distance. Maybe not feeling them per se, but being affected by them on some level. If nothing else, they are reminders to me. Structures break down. Everything is always changing, and I tend to resist change. It is so scary, but it is part of the growth process, isn't it? Breaking down so that something new can come forth. If I am learning anything from Dan, it is to be reminded of the Phoenix coming forth from the ashes. Structures dissolve, new forms are birthed. And maybe that is what happens to us, all through our life here on earth, the growth process. Death and rebirth.

Some news…Gregg had an amazing trip to Oregon in January. He spread some of Dan's ashes at Willamette University where Dan went to college. He spent several days golfing at a course that I think is as close to heaven as Gregg has ever come. He felt Dan very close by. There were even deer waiting by his car one afternoon. I would say, in summary, that Gregg went on a spiritual pilgrimage, and it was more rewarding than he dreamed possible.

Our dear Natalie—what a brave and courageous soul! She has been in New Zealand since late November. She has been traveling and working. (She's worked on farms and most recently cleaning at a hostel.) Making friends wherever she goes. Sprinkling Dan's ashes along some of the most beautiful beaches in the world. Swimming with dolphins. Surely Dan has been with Natalie along some of this journey. As far as we know, Nat plans to return to this country in April (or May?) and to start her graduate program to be a nurse practitioner. I'll keep you posted. For now, she continues to travel, to send us the occasional email, to phone, and to post beautiful, interesting, and joyful photos on her blog website.

Andy has had his challenges that I am not at liberty to mention here. But we are proud of his attitude, his positive outlook on life, and his beautiful and loving family. Of course I'm partial (it is my prerogative as "Nana"!), but Drew, Phoebe, and little Hadley are quite exceptional beings. And Megan is a wonderful mom. She is home schooling them! (Drew would be in kindergarten.)

One thing I did in January was rent a dance studio space one

Saturday morning and gather with a few friends to dance to what I called my "grief CD." I had been playing this CD in my car for many weeks, and crying with it, when I began to feel I really needed to dance to it. The CD, Somewhere Between Heaven and Earth, *is written and performed by an artist, Cindy Bullens, who lost her daughter to cancer. It's a powerful collection of songs. It felt good to move with others, to "grief dance," and I may need to do more of this moving, especially if the disconnection returns. Movement certainly calls to me—it is a powerful way to connect body, mind, and spirit. Writing is pretty good too.*

I wasn't particularly keen to see the movie Avatar, *but a friend wanted to go, and I loved it. There were several aspects that reminded me of Dan. Even seeing the main character moving along in his wheelchair reminded me of Dan in a wheelchair. The main character, Jake, is an unlikely hero. And so was Dan. And what transformed Jake into an awesome gentle warrior? It was Love! The unearthly being who fell in love with him said, at one point, something like, "I see you, and your heart is good." Dan and Natalie "saw" each other, and in that seeing they were transformed. Dan died, but I still say cancer did not win in that "battle." Love won.*

Another powerful sensation for me in the movie was when Jake, paralyzed from the waist down, turns into the "creature." He could suddenly walk again, run, and leap! He went whizzing by, and it was so exhilarating. I like to think of Dan now as being beyond the limitations of his earthly body. That whoever or however he now is, he soars! He is free.

I recently was reminded of a quote on friendship. It's so good I'll include it here.

A friend is one to whom you can pour out the contents of
your heart, chaff and grain alike, knowing that the gentlest
of hands will take and sift it, keep what is worth keeping
and with a breath of kindness, blow the rest away.

> Love and thanks,
> Susan/Susie/Sue

*P.S. I almost forgot to tell you about the first anniversary of Dan's
passing, January 8. It was a magical time. I felt very connected to
that mystical realm. Deep sadness, too—but things happened that
truly felt like messages from beyond. This was enormously comforting and affirming.*

*P.P.S. I have eased out of my bookshop job (kind of scary because
I've worked there over 15 years) but am keeping my Co-op job.
Hopefully I can still sub at the bookshop now and then.*

*P.P.P.S. I have heard that February was a tough month, astrolog-
ically, for a lot of people...hmm. I, for one, am on the lookout for
some joy! May you find some, too.*

*Now it is March 15 and I will include just one story from the first
anniversary of Dan's passing.*

*I awoke on Jan. 8, 2010, to a beautiful day. As I lay in bed I
was thinking about what I would tell grieving people. I thought I
would tell them three things:*

1. Be open
2. Pay attention to the signs
3. Find a way to express the creative energy of grief.

Just then I thought I heard a ringing in my ear. I was very

*annoyed and thought, "Drat! I can't believe I have a ringing in my
ear." But then I realized it was the sound of a tuning fork. And I
had just said to myself in that list, "Pay attention to the signs"…a
tuning fork!*

*You see, the bodyworker who worked so lovingly with Dan to
help him breathe as best as he could had told me that Dan, ever
the musician, had especially loved when she used the tuning forks.
So, I woke on this past January 8 to the sound of a tuning fork.
Dan! And I had almost dismissed it, and missed it altogether. I
wonder how often I have been oblivious to loving nudges from the
universe.*

May/June 2010

Dear Friends,

*I'm back! At least for now, today, this moment. I feel present and
connected, with the urge to write again. It quite amazes me that
some of you have expressed that you really like getting these letters—that you find them helpful and even relevant to your own
life. That is so great! Thank you. Please, if any of you out there
would rather not receive my musings, please do let me know. I
promise not to be offended.*

*I will backtrack a bit. In my last letter I did not have room
to tell you one story that happened on January 7, the day before
the first anniversary of Dan's passing. I had had several dreams
of fires—me trying to put out fires near/around my house. On
January 7, in the afternoon, I emailed a few friends and asked, "I
wonder what all these fire dreams are about?" Later that evening,
because of an unexpected visitor earlier on, I found myself looking
through the book* Animal Speak *by Ted Andrews. I was not consciously looking for anything that I was aware of, and yet I kept*

reading along almost as though I were. Then—at the top of page 24, the word "Fire" caught my eye. This is what it looked like:

THE LESSON OF LIFE, DEATH, AND REBIRTH
MAGIC: CREATION
ELEMENT: FIRE
DIRECTION: SOUTH

And on page 25, I read, "The magic of creation involves learning to use the deaths within your life as opportunities for rebirth.... Fire is destructive as well as creative. It purifies, and it burns away the dross so that the gold can shine forth. It is the mystery of the phoenix who rises from the ashes. Fire is the element of the heart, the center of passions and love that can help us recreate our lives. It is the element of regeneration and resurrection...." (Always with Dan, the words "rebirth, resurrection" keep surfacing.)

That was in January. In February I was aware of shifting. I mentioned it in my last letter. A friendship changed. It caught me off guard and I did not adjust easily to the new reality. I started sleeping poorly. At times I started feeling myself in an altered reality. Where was I? And what were these terrifying feelings that would come over me? About this time I also happened to read an article in The New Yorker *magazine on grief ("Good Grief," by Meghan O'Rourke, January 24, 2010). There was one column in particular that caught my eye.*

In the nineteen-seventies, Colin Murray Parkes, a British psychiatrist and a pioneer in bereavement research, argued that the dominant element of grief was a restless "searching." The heightened physical arousal, anger, and sadness of grief resemble the anxiety that children suffer when they're sepa-rated from their mothers. Parkes, drawing on work by John Bowlby, an early theorist of how human beings form attach-

ments, noted that in both cases—acute grief and children's separation anxiety—we feel alarm because we no longer have a support system we relied on.

It occurred to me, could it be possible? That Dan's dying and now this dropping away of a key friendship—triggered something new in my psyche? Walls of protection shifting? I know that I found myself reliving/feeling very, very, old emotions from when I was a little girl. It felt like a Pandora's box got opened.

So, at times, I simply feel lost in another time. My world feels really small. I can't see the bigger picture, and as a result, what might be just a mole hill could feel like a mountain to me. I will not go into it all here. I will just say it is quite terrifying. I know I even had the thought at one point, "I am not sure I can keep going on like this." Then I remembered that that was what Dan said a few days before he died. When I think about Dan's incredible strength and courage, I renew my resolve to be brave, patient, to have faith. The other really hard part of when I fall into this altered reality is that I feel so separate and cut off from others. It is hard to describe this feeling. Like I am from another planet. The good news is that when I shift back into more like my old self, it feels so good! I used to take "normal" for granted. Whoever thought "normal" could feel so good? I'll take it!

I forgot to mention one other thing that happened right around the time that I was aware of shifting realities…I found out that my last remaining sibling in my large family of origin has lung cancer. I know that this is extremely significant on levels I am barely aware of. Karma, soul/choices, family conditioning/patterns, healing…are just a few words that come to mind.

Here are a few positive things I've been thinking about. Haven't you heard of the theory that if one sense becomes shut down, often another is amplified, e.g., if you lose your sight, then your hearing ability might be quite amazing? It occurred to me just recently, that when I felt my "normal" brain ability working less effectively (and that feels worrisome), maybe another part of my brain is working better than ever? Someone recently told me about a book title—It's Not How Smart You Are, It's How You Are Smart. *I like it! So maybe if you lose one way of thinking, you become better at another way. This week past, I was sitting outside at a café. I saw a car across the street and the thought popped into my head that maybe it was this friend's car. Now, I had never seen what kind of car this friend drove, so it was a very unusual thought to have. Seconds later, this friend's voice jolted me out of my reverie. She was there coming down the sidewalk next to me. We laughed—I told her how I felt I must have manifested her! I told her about seeing the car across the street and wondering if it was her car. But then I saw a man was driving it. She said, "But it is my car. My husband came to pick up our son." So that is a kind of knowing I don't have an explanation for.*

And here is another positive thought. Perhaps when we feel "lost" and we think our brains aren't working properly, and our inner compass has gone kerflooey, maybe there is still some wise part of us that knows exactly what it is doing and is even guiding us, although we may be completely unaware of this. Recently, I was on the floor rewinding a tape in front of a bookshelf in my house. I looked up and saw this book, Healing Through the Dark Emotions: The Wisdom of Grief, Fear, and Despair, *by Miriam Greenspan. I vaguely recall buying the book years ago, but never really reading it. I had forgotten all about it. I opened it up to a section on grief and was amazed at how good it is.*

Even more amazing was the next day when I read the introduction. A key factor for this book coming into existence was the death of the author's son at age two months. She writes, "Aaron's life and death are the ground in which this book is planted. It is his spirit that has guided me through the 13 long years of writing and living that this book entailed." Isn't it quite astonishing that

I should stumble upon this book now? Years ago, when I bought the book, the mention of the death of the author's son would have meant nothing to me. Now, it is a significant connection. Not only does this book look to be quite wonderful (and I noticed when I Googled the author that it indeed received an award), but it also serves as a message to me. This book was a gift to the author, from the grief of her son's death. Often there are gifts in the grieving process...this book is a tangible reminder of that truth.

Another book that landed in my hands with near perfect timing is called The Diamond in Your Pocket—Discovering Your True Radiance, *by Gangaji. What with these old thoughts/feelings coming up and my sense of falling into an altered reality/parallel universe, I am exploring what is real. What is illusion? Who are we? What is the nature of fear and suffering?*

Gangaji writes:

> *When there is an openness to fear, where can it be found? What a strange creature fear is. It exists only when there is resistance to its existence. When you stop and open to what you have resisted throughout time, you find that fear is not fear. Fear is energy. Fear is space. Fear is the Buddha. It is Christ's heart knocking at your door.*

Needless to say, a key word for me these days is "surrender."

And lastly, we return to Dan. In March I asked a trusted intuitive/psychic about Dan, and here is some of what he said:

> *...He is alive, he never has died. He is alive, he has simply shed a form that didn't work anymore. And that is the message for you, to know that when the time comes, you will shed a form that's finished, that's used up, and you will continue your journey in a new form, in a more light-filled form*

as one might say, and will continue that which is of interest and that which is of value to the soul's awakening.

Dan is going to what would be called "school," as you would understand school in earthly terms, and music seems to be the area of expression and learning, and ultimately the bringing of new forms of music to the earth, as that knowledge becomes available and ways for it to be communicated are perfected.

There are also studies in what you would understand as science and in math and also in the realm of technology, which has to do with the communication between minds through technology. This kind of work speaks very strongly to him and will be part of the wavelength of the future and other beings—many, many other beings—who will work to bring this about, even as we speak.

So while I often miss Dan, I do not worry about him. He is still doing music! And maybe if he gets a little time off from his studies, just maybe he could give me a little help now and then, when I'm traveling through these dark emotions. Dear Dan.

Gregg, Andy and family, Natalie—everyone is really doing pretty well. May you find peace and joy in the stillness of your being. I hope I do, too!

Love,
Susan/Susie/Sue

P.S. The Dan Humphrey Music Scholarship went to two students this year, one of whom Dan gave piano and saxophone lessons to! They will be attending summer music camps.

September 22, 2010

Dear Friends,

Hello! Hello! It's been a while...a couple of you have egged me on to send an update. So here I am. A few reasons I haven't written sooner are: 1. It's expensive. 2. Sometimes my writing self just isn't there, and it's hard to organize my thoughts. 3. Self-doubt—do I have anything worthwhile to share? That's a big question.

Right away I will say again that I don't know a thing. Sometimes I am not even sure what is real or illusion. But I can share my experience with you—and maybe there will be some small nuggets of gold among the "garbage."

Since I last wrote not too much has changed. I do have good days. They seem like miracles—days that in the past I would have considered just "normal." It turns out normal is great. And I still have not-so-good days. It is really hard to talk about those experiences because the truth is, my life is good. At times these painful thoughts/feelings/fears just seem to sweep over me, coming out of nowhere. They are all in my mind! Sometimes I worry about mental illness (which seems to run in just about all families), but a friend who has worked with numerous grieving families assures me that these up-and-down mood swings (with up-and-down thoughts) are part of the grieving process, even though it is now over a year and a half since Dan's passing. Sometimes I believe her, sometimes I have my doubts.

Interestingly, a lot of my attention for the past year and a half has gone to looking at the crawlspaces in our house. What is going on down there? And how can we improve the drainage/moisture problem, the heating, etc. It mirrors my own inner house, where the shock of Dan's dying has set things loose. Old beliefs, memories, limited vision, painful experiences/feelings...they've all gotten shaken up somehow. I think I mentioned in my last letter that an

important word for me was "surrender." Another one I am now
to be working with is "integration." This is work at a foundational
level, just like the work we've been doing to our house at a foundational level. Looking at the dark, dark areas we usually prefer to
ignore.

Briefly I need to tell you that my last remaining sibling, Tim,
passed away September 4 from lung cancer. We were not particularly close, but we became closer, being the last two alive, and he
would call me every few weeks. I spent a little time with him in
July, a trip I dreaded but that ended up somehow having a healing quality to it—some grace. Tim reminded me so much of our
father. I thought about the genes we inherit. I thought about the
little boy Tim must have been long before I was born, and I found
myself at times feeling quite tender toward him. Tim could be
extremely difficult, so this tenderness caught me by surprise—an
unexpected gift.

Two books have been very important to me. I mentioned one of
them to you in my last letter—Healing Through the Dark Emotions, by Miriam Greenspan. This is one I found on my very own
shelf when I spotted the word "healing." It took me a long time to
read, and it is not for the faint of heart. But it is incredibly rich
and dives deep. I will try to include in this letter the author's story
of her family's pet snake, Sam. It is such a powerful message to
trust this process. Her writing goes from the very personal out to
the larger world. It is all connected. A seminal work indeed.

The other book was brought to my attention while visiting Tim.
One of his friends was reading it. Mindsight, by Daniel Siegel,
offers the good news that no matter what our genes are, our past
experiences, traumas, etc., the neural pathways in our brains can
change—even in someone as old as 90! It is fascinating and hopeful. What the books both share, among other things, is a reference
to Albert Einstein, who coined the phrase "the optical delusion
of our consciousness." It turns out Einstein wrote about this in

response to a rabbi who had written him shortly after the acciden-
tal death of one of his (the rabbi's) daughters. My antennae went
up; there it is again—the theme of the loss of a child.

One day—a not-so-good day—I noticed a folded paper on my
printer. It turned out to be a sermon a friend gave me years ago
that her sister had written. I found it on Aug. 21, and the sermon
was dated Aug. 20, 2006. It is quite likely that it had fallen onto
my printer (out of the desk drawer) on Aug. 20. I pay attention
now to things like dates and numbers. It was as though it had
surfaced for me to read now (I had never read it back when it was
first given to me). The sermon was called "Holy Wisdom," and
most significantly, it ended with a Rilke poem. That is a strong
Dan connection, because he did his senior thesis on Rilke. The
poem ends with the line "Give me your hand." And honestly, on
that day when I was feeling a bit lost in some sort of a brain fog, it
was as though Dan, or some other helping spirit, was reaching out
a hand to me and reminding me that I was not alone.

Just a brief update on the others. Natalie is enrolled in the
Nurse Practitioner Program at UVM. She is a wondrous star in
our life. Gregg continues to be passionate about his work with
students in the Teacher Education Department. He also delights
in cooking, golf, and bluegrass music-making. He did have a frus-
trating Dan dream this week where he was trying to reach Dan by
phone but was not able to.

I have been reflecting this week that, as I look back over my
life, meeting and marrying Gregg is the best thing that happened
to me. Interestingly, I am the only one of six siblings who had
children—children who were lucky enough to have a great dad
like Gregg. Andy's family is busy-busy—with an almost-seven-
year-old, a five-year-old, and a one-year-old. We will be going to
Andy's family (Traverse City, MI) for Thanksgiving.

On the very day I started seeing a therapist, I came across this
poem, "The Medicine Way," in a pile of old papers as I was looking

for something else. It came to me, like an unexpected blessing, and I just love it. I will include a copy for you.

I could be going crazy…and losing my mind and soul. But on my better days, I choose to hope that I am perhaps like that snake, Sam (see story below). Dying to the old. And that just maybe, someday, I will be "more lively, beautiful, and alert than ever"—a born-again me! Thank you for being there.

Love,

Susan/Susie/Sue

P.S. I am starting to meditate!

The Medicine Way

Let Light enfold me
That my inward eye may see clearly
The Path that lies ahead.
Let my mind be opened up
That I may recognize
The signposts along the Way.

Grant me the wisdom
That comes from understanding
The true from the false.
And guide my steps
So that should I falter or stumble,
Tripped by my former beliefs
That blind me still
I may go forward with courage
And with the determination
Which persistence bears.

Let me be embraced
With the Love by which
The whole Creation is moved.
The very Essence with which
All things are held together
Dependent yet independent,
Whole yet individuated.
In which all are my relatives.

Let me know the way
That is the Beauty Way
The beautiful way
Where all who will
May Walk in Beauty
And where the end of the Path
Is but a new beginning
To my infinity.
And every new beginning
Another ever-present moment
In Eternity.

—*Anonymous*

Excerpt from Healing Through the Dark Emotions: The Wisdom
of Grief, Fear, and Despair, *by Miriam Greenspan:*

*Sam was a bright green with darker markings. We never did
find a way to detect snake gender and decided, by fiat, to
make Sam a girl and give her a masculine-sounding name
that could also pass as a nickname for Samantha. Sam
(whose gender identity was no doubt terribly confused) slid
around her cage gracefully, looping in and out of the holes*

in the wooden structure in her fish-tank home. She slept a lot but always seemed interested in being taken out to have a look around. Every few days, Sam ate three to five small guppies for dinner. We'd watch in amazed, horrified fascination as she swallowed each fish whole and the bulge slid down her throat. (Do snakes have throats?) Sam was active and energetic. She loved to be touched and enjoyed circling herself around Anna's neck like an emerald necklace as Anna did her chores.

Then, one day, Sam became more subdued than usual. She wasn't swooshing around in her snake house. She seemed sluggish, and her appetite was suppressed. She ate poorly and then not at all, the fish lying belly up in Sam's water dish. We worried and watched over her.

After more than a week of this depressed behavior, Sam seemed on her last snake-legs. Her bright green skin, so alive and vibrant, had turned brown and dull. She lay on the floor of the cage, motionless. "She's dead," I thought. Feeling a pang of sorrow that deepened as I thought about announcing the news to Anna, I rushed off to work.

Several hours later, I returned—and Sam was gone! There on the cage bottom was a perfectly formed snakeskin, its zigzag design intact but hollow. The snakeskin lay there, a translucent sculpture—but where was Sam? Taking the top off the cage, I picked up the wooden snake house with its circular holes in which Sam did her morning exercises, and gasped as Sam jutted out of a hole, leaping and slithering around the cage at breakneck speed—more vital and full of energy than when we first took her home from the pet shop. Sam's little red tongue darted in and out of her jaws. Her eyes sparkled. Her skin was a brighter hue of green. Having shed her skin, she was more lively, beautiful, and alert than ever. She was a born-again snake.

Despair's alchemy is this kind of transformation. There is a descent to a state of death in life. We look and feel dead, but something is happening under the skin—if we let it. The mask of the old self's dying—a harbinger of resurrection.

FERNGLADE

2011–2016

"Everything I do is stitched with its color."

—W. S. Merwin, "Separation"

April 17, 2011

Hello dear friends!

It has been a long time since I have written to you. I wasn't sure if I was at the end of my letter writing to you as a group, but here I am again. I hope I will be able to share a little bit of where I've been—and I hope it may be of interest, and maybe even helpful, to someone out there.

My sharings probably won't come out in chronological order, but hopefully it will all make sense. I know I've said it in the past, and it is worth saying again, that the older I get, the more I seem to realize that I don't know anything. I surely am curious, but I also know that much in life will always remain a mystery. We just do our best to muddle along in our search for truth, justice, and meaning. I have had a recurring image of myself at the end of my life…I am given a life review, and in that process I realize that most of what I thought was true really wasn't. We are so limited by our thoughts and perceptions. Oh, the stories we tell ourselves!

It was at the end of February, 2010, that I felt this frightening shift. I remember feeling extremely disoriented and as though I had slipped into an altered reality. One night, awake in bed, I felt as though I were seeing all the horror in the world at once—murders, wars, crime, confusion, people hurting one another. It felt absolutely terrifying and I prayed, saying, "Dear Lord, please forgive them, they know not what they do…." That is how it seemed to me, that most people wanted to do the right thing but we were lost. That included me. I remember thinking that if I totally lose my bearings, to just remember a few simple guidelines—be kind, and treat others as you would want them to treat you. The problem seemed to be in my mind—I know I even said to myself, "My mind is killing me."

Last Christmas was extremely hard. It was not so much because of missing Dan. In fact, I was missing "missing Dan," if that makes any sense. I was pretty much preoccupied with my own terrors, with trying to stay sane, with wanting to do the "right" thing at all times, but often not having a clear sense of what that was. It was as though my inner compass, which had guided me so wisely and safely for most of my life, was somehow malfunctioning. I told a few friends that at times I felt unsure if I had just dropped a knitting stitch or killed someone! Not being able to differentiate between the severity of different situations left me feeling pretty anxious the whole time. And sometimes old feelings would come over me out of nowhere.

Christmas Eve I reached a new low. I was reading an older book called A Book of Angels, *and I got to a part where the author is talking about demonic possession. Reading her description I was convinced that that must be what had happened to me. I felt absolutely worthless to the core and unredeemable. I mean, what could be worse than being demonically possessed? Fortunately, I read on, and later the author says the three women she's met whom she considered "possessed" all shared one trait. They were each incredibly beautiful physically. Well, I know I look okay, but I am definitely not physically beautiful! Yay! I was so relieved. Maybe I wasn't possessed after all.*

At a grief group for bereaved parents, as others shared how much they missed their child who had died, I realized I was not so much missing Dan right then; oddly enough, I was missing my mother at some very deep level.

This missing of my mother, and the feelings that would sometimes come over me of "no one is there," led me to look for Christine. Christine had looked after me when I was little. All of my large family has died, but it turns out I was able to reconnect with Christine, who lives in Chester, Nova Scotia, where my family once lived. She is turning 88 in May! She remembers meeting me in the hospital when I was just a few days old. I have talked to her several times now and knitted her a pair of socks for her birthday. I can't change the past, but I can honor and be grateful to all who helped me stay alive.

I loved the movie The King's Speech *and saw it on a day when I was feeling good. My favorite line was one I imagined most of the viewers hardly noticed. I even grabbed a pen out of my purse and jotted it down as I sat in that darkened theater. The speech therapist/friend says to the king, "You no longer need to be afraid of what you were afraid of when you were five."*

I am just realizing that there is far more I want to share with you than I can possibly fit in these pages—even if I write with really small print. I am just going to have to pick and choose, and leave some things out.

Over these past few months, I occasionally reread passages from Healing Through the Dark Emotions. *The author talked about being in a long-term women's group—a group for befriending the dark emotions. I wanted to be in such a group and, on a good day, I thought I could actually maybe start such a group. But then my brain would switch again, and it seemed an impossible task. In telling someone about this, I wrote, "I would consider such a group as also a support group and a spiritual group, that in this befriending, we are supporting each other on our spiritual journeys, to work through the muck, so that we can know our 'larger' selves, know ourselves at a soul level, and serve the world with those gifts each of us has but that are so often clouded by all the crap."*

In her chapter on grief, Miriam Greenspan writes, "The simultaneous shattering of ego and expansion of consciousness is a common experience for people who are grieving.... Descending, the heart breaks open and the ego loses its moorings.... We are rarely counseled to understand that it is precisely the surrender of the normal self that makes grief transformative.... In a sense, grief is a birth process from ego to spirit." Also she writes, "Grief in the present taps into the deep reservoir of grief from the past."

With my inner compass no longer feeling trustworthy and old feelings at times overwhelming me, there were definitely times when I could see I was "needy." And this felt shameful. Somewhere in my belief system was the idea that neediness equals abandonment; e.g., if you are needy, others will leave you. And I still have confusion around this. On January 9, 2011, the day after the second anniversary of Dan's passing, Emily (the wonderful interim minister at the Unitarian-Universalist Church) touched on this in her sermon. She said, "Inner work is not dead-end navel gazing; self-care is not self-indulgent; and self-love is not narcissistic.... We've been taught that we're not supposed to say anything when we're in need. In fact, most of us have been taught that compared to others, we are not in need. We use the knowledge of our relative economic privilege to discount our own pain and suffering, which are equally real.... If we can't say anything when we're in need, we are disconnected from our true selves." Thank you, Emily.

I always appreciate Pema Chödrön's wisdom, and in her book The Places That Scare You, *she writes about the importance of "maitri" or loving-kindness. She writes, "Staying with pain without loving-kindness is warfare." A light bulb went off in my head when I read that! I had been trying to be open and accepting of whatever came up for me (e.g., not to resist...), but I could recognize that I was completely lacking in loving-kindness for myself at this point, and trying to welcome pain was warfare. And I happened to hear an interview on the podcast "Sounds True" with the author and clinical psychologist Tara Brach. She said that without inner resources meditation can be retraumatizing for some people. It is not helpful to relive terrifying feelings from childhood without first developing a safe space and resources with which to handle those strong emotions. She talked about what was going on in the brain, too. I asked my therapist to please help me establish some inner resources, an inner place of safety.*

I was pretty worn down by the end of January. I had had at least three occasions of extreme self-attacks, as I called them. I still had good days, times when I really felt like "myself" (whoever that is), and could think clearly and feel safe and content. But those times would last for a day or less. I might start the day not-too-bad-off, but then sometime after lunch I might notice when my brain would start to feel different, like a darkness coming on, and I'd be back in this other reality. My therapist asked me once something about what I wanted, or what is it I hoped for. After I got home what came to my mind was that I just wanted to be glad to be alive. It was as simple as that.

I figured if that could be in place then everything else, my life purpose, how to be of service in the world, my relationships, all would fall into place as well. Again, something just did not feel right in my brain. A connection would be there one moment, and then be gone the next. With relationships/friendships it was as though our past history suddenly got erased. It's not that I ever forgot who people were, but suddenly something was different. And then on another day, the connection was back. I did wonder if perhaps I was experiencing beginning symptoms of Alzheimer's. Sometimes I could feel forgiveness and support should I flounder and make a "mistake"; other times I simply could not feel any safety net that might catch me.

Now it is April 22, and I am finally to the part of this letter that I have been looking forward to—telling you the good news! In February (2011), I went to my regular doctor and he prescribed Zoloft for me. (I started with Paxil but had a bad experience.) I started with a very, very small dose and slowly increased over time with no negative side effects. The first thing I noticed was that I began to sleep better. I could actually wake up at 4 a.m., even get up to use the bathroom and then go back to sleep. Sometimes I barely wake up in the night at all. Lots of dreaming....

I thought maybe I was feeling a little better; then on March 21, the first day of spring (?), I knew something was really different.

I just felt solidly here. It is hard to describe. And then the next day was good, and the next, and the next. I could hardly believe it. I wanted to email you all to tell you about this miracle, but I was afraid I might jinx it. The whole week was good—in fact, even though some days now are better than others, I have not once (knock wood) returned to that worst place. What I especially noticed was that the hypercritical voices that seemed like they were almost trying to kill me simply stopped. I couldn't even remember the bad things they were saying about me. The sense of relief, and release, from such relentless self-criticism was quite extraordinary.

One morning was especially amazing. The world seemed to sparkle to me. It was as though all my worries and fears lifted—I felt so light. And what remained was joy. And such love! I felt love for everyone and such gratitude for my parents, too. The feeling I had was somehow familiar, like a memory. I thought to myself that I had felt this way before, a long, long time ago. When I had been feeling at my worst, I sometimes would say to myself, "My basic goodness is always there; it's just that sometimes it gets covered up and I can't feel it." Well, on this magical morning, I think that is what I was in touch with: my basic goodness. I kept saying to myself, "Oh, my God, this is just amazing!" And I felt that this basic goodness was at the core of everyone, but like for me, it often gets covered up. It was a wondrous realization—to feel this truth, to actually feel it, not just to think it.

Thinking about what a holy experience I had that morning reminded me of this brain scientist I'd heard about. She had a stroke that caused her left brain to be temporarily non-functional. Working with her right brain, she experienced such peace, bliss, and oneness. I thought, "I have to find her book." I did (at The Vermont Book Shop), and I have almost finished reading it. It is called My Stroke of Insight. *I am now very interested in how our experience of "God," of the mystical realm, relates to our brains and our brain chemicals and neural pathways.*

I am still a little fragile-feeling—not completely confident that this new stability will be long-lasting, but I surely do hope so. Dan wanted so much to stay alive. I knew that the best way I could ever honor Dan would be to love my life, to appreciate being alive. And I do. I am feeling glad to be alive!

It's true the only thing that makes any sense is kindness and compassion. You all have been amazing role models for me. Thank you so very, very much.

xxx,
Susan/Susie/Sue

P.S. Gregg, Andy and family, and Natalie are all doing well, and I hope you are too! Isn't spring the most lovely time of year? I find it very therapeutic when I get to hang around my grandchildren, who are now ages seven, five, and one year and eight months old. They still live in Michigan.

P.P.S. The music scholarship given in Dan's honor continues. The first recipient graduates this year and has been accepted into the Crane School of Music for music education. He credits his experience at the jazz camp (thanks to the scholarship) for catapulting him in that direction.

October 2, 2011

Dear Friends,

I have actually been wanting to write you for quite some time. A month? Two months? Time is still very strange for me, and seems to pass all too quickly by. I have been feeling a need to write you one last letter. Yes, I am one to have a P.S. and a P.P.S. and a

P.P.P.S. *in my writing, so I am not saying I will never write to you all, as a group, ever again—but I feel a sense of closure somehow. I started writing you shortly after Dan's cancer diagnosis, and now it is four years later.*

First and foremost, thank you for being there for me in so many ways—even at times when I was unable to know you were there. Thank you for having faith in me, and for sharing your own journey with me. Thank you for forgiving me when I could not fully reciprocate your kindness; sometimes connections just evaporated and it was hard to remember who I was or who anyone else was. I understand about getting older and forgetting names, or what I've already said, or you've said. But the forgetting I'm talking about is a much deeper disconnect.

As I last wrote you, the major turn-around came for me on March 21 of this year. Ironic that it was the first day of spring. Maybe it was time for something to finally shift in me; maybe the antidepressant (Zoloft) I had started taking finally kicked in. Who knows? The memory of how crazy and afraid I felt from about February 2010 until March 2011 is still vivid enough that every day when I check in with myself and feel someone there, I am incredibly grateful. It still has a miraculous quality for me—living this ordinary and extraordinary life, and feeling like an okay person. I guess the downside might be that I have very few ambitions these days. Being released from the grips of that mostly constant terror and relentless self-criticism, a whole new world has opened up for me. I make my bed and do the dishes, I am happy. I work as a cashier at the Co-op, read books, watch TV, I am happy. I share meals and conversation with Gregg and with friends, I tend the garden and vacuum the house, I am happy. I stop to take pictures, I make cards, I visit Andy and his family, I am happy. I snuggle with our dog, Buddy, I go to group meetings, meet new people, I knit and run errands in town, I am happy. And again—not knowing why I am feeling so good, I appreciate each moment of this sanity. For all I know, the dark cloud of despair could descend on me at any moment. So it is about this moment, this now. I feel good, I feel like a worthwhile person. I am happy. Isn't it a wondrous thing?

Over the summer, I continued to water Dan's tree, which has grown tall and beautiful. We hope to have a plaque up either before winter or in the springtime. I think of Dan all the time in one way or another—he's just part of me now—although I don't feel him around as much as I used to, fewer "signs," if you know what I mean. I figure it's because he's busy doing other things now. Most recently I experienced him at Weybridge School. I went in for a nighttime meeting and heard the piano playing. It sounded like it could have been Dan. It was a student playing, now a sixth-grader, who had been in the first-grade class Dan was helping teach as an aide when he was diagnosed with cancer. I introduced myself, and this young man, Oziah, looked up and said, "I remember Dan; he was my favorite teacher." At that moment my heart opened, and I could feel Dan there. A holy moment.

Natalie is now into the second year of her nurse practitioner program—she is studying to take the boards this month. If she passes the exam, she will be an RN. Poor Natalie—I don't know how she puts up with me and my camera, because I am always wanting to take pictures of her. For me she is still stunningly beautiful, with a soul-beauty neither words nor photos can truly capture. I am so grateful to Dan for bringing her into our lives.

Andy and family are doing well. We are going to spend our first Christmas together in Michigan this year. Drew will be eight, Phoebe six, and Hadley two! I don't know if it's because they are homeschooled, but they all still have an innocence and sweetness that is just a joy to be around.

Sometimes, besides feeling happy and fortunate, I get an excited feeling inside…like something good is waiting for me, or I am going to make a wonderful discovery. I have recently had my hair cut and am encouraging it to be curly. Like Phoebe's, it is naturally curly. People have been telling me it makes me look younger. And the funny thing is—I am feeling younger—like parts of me long buried and forgotten are resurfacing.

I inherited some unexpected money from my brother Tim, who passed away last year. Tim really enjoyed golf and playing golf with Gregg. Gregg has never been to Europe, and neither of us has been to Scotland, where my mother's ancestors hail from, so one of my fantasies is to take Gregg to Scotland. He will play golf there, and we will toast Tim!

As I said—the "Dan moments" are less frequent, but there are still times when something odd happens that makes me sit up and pay attention. When these things happen I try to remember to write them down, with the date they occurred. But I forgot to write down the one I am going to tell you about, so I am not sure when it happened. I think maybe a couple of months ago.

Early on, I mentioned to you that Dan's message seemed to be about resurrection and rebirth. Right from the beginning there was that symbol the deer left in the snow shortly after his passing and cremation. It looked like the infinity sign, or the number 8. Well, a month or two ago on the side of my computer screen the name Tara Vanacore popped up. Tara was a friend of Dan's. After he died, she told me of Dan sending her a written piece he was working on (I think he was looking for constructive critique; it was something about his running experience and meeting up with a deer). This exchange he had with Tara was several years back, maybe in college, or shortly after.

Anyway, Tara and I exchanged a couple of emails after Dan's dying, but when I saw her name on my computer, I thought maybe she was writing me again, although I couldn't imagine why she would get in touch with me now. When I clicked on her name, what came up was not a current message from her but a copy of an Easter sermon she had sent me from April of 2009. I had

*read it at the time, but when it reappeared "accidentally," I knew
I was supposed to read it again. And there it was—the message
about resurrection and renewal—exactly what I have been feeling!
Thank you, Tara, for the original email, and thank you Dan/Mystery for putting it up on my computer screen once again.*

*Remember how in one of my letters I told you how, when I
blew out candles on a cake, my wish was always something about
wanting to feel more love? (Not to be more loved, but to feel more
loving.) I never really had the right words, but I knew what I
meant. This summer in Maine, I found words posted in a bathroom at a whole health center and immediately recognized that
they were the "wishing words" I had been searching for. They are,
"May love brighten in and through me." I am so happy to have
these words—I hold them close, and repeat them often.*

And so—a new cycle begins....

Much love to all,
Susan/Susie/Sue

*P.S. I may be in a time of integration and deep appreciation. That
said, I give you this quote by Florida Scott-Maxwell: "You need
only claim the events of your life to make yourself yours. When
you truly possess all you have been and done...you are fierce with
reality."*

*P.P.S. Late breaking news (October 9). Natalie passed the board
exam and is now officially an RN!*

SOMETIME IN 2012, I had a conversation with God. I remember
where I was when it happened, but not whether there was anything in particular that brought it on. I was sitting in my car, in
downtown Middlebury, and suddenly I imagined a scenario. It

was the end of my life, and there I was having a life review with God.

I started to tell God about some of the ways I thought I'd been a help in the world. God was attentive and polite, nodding occasionally. And then he said, "Did you love your life?" I then proceeded to tell him a few more of my better moments, while also confessing to some things I wasn't too proud of.

God listened patiently. He didn't exactly yawn, but once again he said, "And did you love your life?" It took me a while, but it finally dawned on me that the God of my imagination wasn't all that interested in a litany of good deeds and shortfalls. What he most wanted to hear about was how I delighted in my life! He wanted to hear all about the twists and turns of the journey, the amazing synchronicities, how just when I thought my life was over, something unexpected and wonderful would come along. He wanted to hear how deepest darkness over time transformed to light, how angst and confusion led to a dawning of new understanding, how loneliness and despair were speckled with moments of such sheer grace. In the end, he wanted to know if I'd been able to see that all the twists and turns, the glorious along with the unbearably painful, were part of a beautiful tapestry.

This imaginary conversation with God continues inside of me. And while I do still aspire to do, and be, a bit of good in this world, I want it not to come from a place of neediness. Nor from a sense of duty or obligation, nor from guilt or ego. I want it to come from fullness, from a cup running over, from my own innate inner joy—the joy that I believe each of us is born with and can tap into.

And I take seriously the instructions of the flight attendant who advises passengers to secure their own oxygen mask first, before helping others.

Most of all, when I die and meet up with my maker, I want to be able to say, "Thank you so very much for *all* of it. I loved my life!"

December 12, 2012

12/12/12

Dear Friends,

I have been feeling a desire to write you. Also, a few of you have told me you miss my letters. When I sat down today with pen and paper in hand and realized the date, I knew it was just the perfect time to connect with you all.

Dave Brubeck died exactly a week ago, one day before his 92nd birthday. Apparently there have been some nice messages on Facebook about Dan and Dave (I'm not on Facebook). I pulled out the photos Natalie took of Dan meeting Dave and talking to him backstage. You may recall that Dan actually wrote Dave just a few days before his passing. Well, Dan dictated the letter and Natalie wrote it. His last paragraph said, "I'll do my very best to warm up the band in heaven so that the celebration will be ready for you and Iola. In the meantime, keep going with your phenomenal work. Love, Dan."

After Dan died, Dave wrote me a letter on a sheet of yellow paper from a legal pad that he signed, "Love from Dave and Iola" (Dave's wife). In that letter he commented on how much he enjoyed the CD Dan had sent him—the CD of Dan playing many of his own songs as well as Brubeck's songs. At the end of the letter Dave writes, "He is keeping a corner in heaven for us so we can all join together in a great celebration, and of course, a promised two-piano concert." So that is what I have been picturing all week—Dan with a great big grin on his face, sitting at a piano and looking over to Brubeck, who is sitting nearby at his piano. They are just about to begin making a joyful noise together!

Yesterday Natalie called. She was calling from the airplane— the airplane that is taking her to India! Natalie has one year left in her three-year program to become a Nurse Practitioner. She finished her final exam of the semester and now has a month off. She is going to India to attend her friend Gale's wedding. Gale knew Dan growing up, and Gale is the one who introduced Natalie to Dan when they happened to see him at the Co-op, where Dan was working in the produce department. Gale is marrying an Indian, and Natalie is on another of her great traveling adventures.

Also, recently, the plaque for Dan's tree at the Middlebury College Snow Bowl was finally put in place. It looks a little out of proportion; the post it is on is slightly larger than I expected. But as the tree grows, and the post weathers, I think it will look good. It is a simple plaque—Dan's name and dates—but ends with a quote that makes it unique, because it is the last line of a poem Dan wrote and gave to us on a Christmas Eve. The last line is, "A smiling heart is all one needs."

This has been a year of digging and planting for me—"playing" on our land. It started one Sunday afternoon late last fall when I suddenly got the urge to clear the brush at the edge of our yard by the side of the brook. I worked and worked at it, even clearing brush off a bit of land in the brook that is like a teeny island. All week I worked on it. Then I dragged over some wood that was left from a walkway we once had; it made a perfect bridge to the island.

I thought I would plant a few daffodils there for Dan. It was so late in the season, December, that it was hard to find any. But I found one package of white bulbs. I wouldn't normally have bought white ones, but that's all there were. Driving home, I noticed they were called "Mount Hood Narcissus." Mount Hood is where Dan snowboarded in Oregon when he went to college there. In fact, he described his "perfect day" to Natalie as the day he went snowboarding on Mount Hood. So it was another "Dan moment." And thus the island became "Daffodil Island."

From spring through summer, I planted a total of 25 bushes on our property. Granted, some of them were small, but I loved the physical exertion and the sense of pride in my accomplishment. I felt grateful to my body for being able to do this work. (I didn't appreciate getting poison ivy twice!)

In one area where I planted, I had to dig up lots of little sumacs, and in all this digging I unearthed the remains of a plastic kiddie pool—one that Dan had splashed around in as a toddler. It is decorated with Cookie Monster, whom he loved. I couldn't quite dispose of it completely, but dragged it off to the side under the branches of fir trees we planted long ago in the part of our yard we call the "fairy forest." It is such a great reminder of all the layers in our property, the layers in our lives.

We have lived here since 1978, and our land and house hold many stories. One of the new stories is "Jay's lilac." This fall we had a buried oil tank removed, and in the process, the excavator, an older man, moved a lilac for me. When he came back again, I asked if he could possibly move another one. But later I realized it would mean first cleaning the contaminated residue off his machine, so I told him please not to bother.

But by then, we had shared stories. I had learned that his son, who was in his forties, had died the very same year Dan died, and from a very rare cancer. As John, the excavator, and I stood there together, we could feel our sons around us. When I got home later that day, the lilac had been moved. And now I shall forever think of it as "Jay's lilac," after John's son.

This summer we rented a little place on Lake Michigan near Andy, Megan, and the grandchildren. We had a wonderful time. We especially enjoyed having the older two kids spend the night with us, one at a time. The first day we were there, I had a holy *moment. We were checking things out, and I'd gone down to the little beach area below and was looking out to the water. Suddenly my eyes just filled with tears, tears of such sweet gladness, and the thought that passed through my head was, "I never thought I would ever feel such happiness again," and the joy and love I felt just made me cry. It was so deep and went back so far, way before Dan, to my childhood. That feeling happened once more on that trip, and several times since then.*

Gregg is doing well—just as passionate as ever about his work, his students, his bluegrass music, his golf. He is loving life and also looking forward to retiring in the next few years. We talk about that Scotland trip. And others too. And we are also new parents— we have two new kittens, who are now about four months old. We love them dearly! The first thing Gregg says when he comes home each day is, "Where are the kids?" I have been surprised at the motherly, nurturing feelings these kittens have awakened in me. When they were tiny, I think I would have nursed them if I could have. Which leads me to mention a dream a friend had of me. She didn't even know about the kittens. Here is her dream:

How surprised I was to discover that my dear friend, Susan, was pregnant and soon to deliver! It was a beautiful Indian summer day when I arrived at her house. I was not alone— for all of the women who had attended "Susan's Circle" when Dan was first diagnosed were also coming. Everyone brought food, and I was in charge of receiving it. We all lifted Susan up with our fingertips as she gave birth to a beautiful baby girl named Danielle. We were all so happy for her.

This dream was such a gift to me because, besides the kittens, I almost feel this has been a year of giving birth to myself. I don't know if this is a gift of being 60 years old, or if it is a gift from living through the depths of despair. I know gratitude in a way I never dreamed possible. My life, in retrospect, seems incredibly rich and privileged. It surprises me that I think of my original family, my parents and all five of my siblings now on the "other side," almost every day, with an almost overwhelming love and appreciation. I have retrieved so many snippets of memories this year, good memories—memories of myself as curious, courageous, funny, loving and at home with everyone. I love so deeply this little one I had forgotten about.

In closing, I share with you a poem that has spoken to me this whole year past. I discovered that the poet Derek Walcott lived for much of his life in Trinidad. Tobago is where I lived when I was younger—Trinidad and Tobago are considered one country now.

May this be a time of joy and true thanksgiving, of wonder and delight, for all of you dear ones, for in truth, we are so incredibly blessed with this gift of life!

Much love,
Susan/Susie/Sue

Love After Love

The time will come
when, with elation
you will greet yourself arriving
at your own door, in your own mirror
and each will smile at the other's welcome,

and say, sit here. Eat.
You will love again the stranger who was your self.
Give wine. Give bread. Give back your heart
to itself, to the stranger who has loved you

135

all your life, whom you ignored
for another, who knows you by heart.
Take down the love letters from the bookshelf,

the photographs, the desperate notes,
peel your own image from the mirror.
Sit. Feast on your life.

—Derek Walcott

*P.S. It has been a little more than five years since my first letter in
July 2007, written shortly after the healing circle, where we sang,*

> *Make new friends, but keep the old,
> one is silver and the other is gold.
> The circle is round, it has no end,
> that's how long I'm going to be your friend.*

*Over the past five years I have made new friends, and I love both
my silver and gold friends.*

December 24, 25, 26, 2013

Dear Friends,

*Hello! It has been five years since I sat down in this very same
room, with the CD* Lux Aeterna *playing in the background, writing to you of the sacred time in our lives as Dan moved ever closer
to leaving his earthly life.*

*That Christmas Eve night, 2008, Natalie, her parents, Gregg,
and I gathered at Dan and Nat's apartment in Middlebury. Andy
had left days earlier, to head home to his family in Michigan. We*

started to hear a bell ringing in the distance. Then we realized it was getting louder and closer, until it was right on our doorstep! It looked like Santa had arrived! But on closer inspection we could see it was actually Dan's friend Brian, who had come to bring good cheer—in full costume. Nat's family went off to the Catholic church for mass; Gregg and I went somewhere, too.

When we returned, I could see that Dan and Brian had been in a deep conversation. There were tears in Dan's eyes, and I was so grateful to Brian for being the listening presence just when Dan needed it the most. Dan had not been sleeping well (he could not lie back and had to sleep sitting up), but that Christmas Eve he slept better than he had in days. It was a bittersweet Christmas—full of merriment, and sadness, too. The night of the 25th we played games, and Dan and Natalie played duets (he on keyboard, she on flute). Dan continued playing piano well past midnight. We knew the end of Dan's life was near—yet he was still with us. Each moment was precious beyond measure.

Brian gave me a book after Dan died. He may have given it to me in January, or it might have been in May after the service we held celebrating Dan's life. Anyway, when someone heard I was going to Ireland, she asked if I'd read the book Anam Cara *by John O'Donohue, and I remembered it was the book Brian had given me. I thought for sure I'd read it, but when I found it on my bookshelf and looked more closely, it appeared I had not. So I took it to Ireland with me, read some of it there, and then finished it recently at home—about five years after it was first given to me. The timing could not have been more perfect.*

Ireland? You are asking...yes! Through a set of unusual circumstances, I found myself on a weeklong bus tour of Ireland, the week before Thanksgiving. It would be a pilgrimage of sorts, I told friends—just Dan and I were going, and I didn't even need to buy him a ticket! I did take a few of his ashes with me, to sprinkle wherever I felt called to do so. It was a wonderful trip. And I rec-

ommend it to everyone. So much history, ancient history, beautiful surroundings, and people with a wicked sense of humor.

Our bus driver, John, was the best! I was overcome with emotion on several occasions, hardly able to believe that I was in this special place—traveling around with Dan, my helpers on the invisible side, ancestors, and a bus-load of total strangers. It was a whirlwind tour, just one week. But I am told magic can happen, and often does, in Ireland. Between you and me, I half believe it may have been just a week in normal American time, but it was much longer in magical Ireland time!

Some places we stayed for two nights, some just for one night. The first thing I looked for in my room when I arrived was the little plug-in pot for making tea! And that became a daily ritual— just me in my room sipping tea—no matter how hectic the rest of the day might be.

I loved being on a tour where everything was planned by someone else. And I relished, also, being on my own, with time and quiet to listen for guidance from the other side. I notice that I am often living my days now in what I would name a "call and response" relationship with the world. And even though I am usually on my own when engaged in this communication, I feel I am not alone, but truly "accompanied" in the best sense of the word.

One surprise message I received on the trip was almost halfway into it. We were staying, for just one night, at a castle. Yes, a castle! Ashford Castle. I felt like I'd been dropped into the set of Downton Abbey. *On the back of the door to my luxurious bathroom there were two bathrobes hanging, complete with terry slippers wrapped in plastic. I do not know where this impulse came from (I was not going to wear the bathrobe), but I found myself lifting the collar slightly so I could read the label. It said "VERMONT" in big block letters! I practically fell over laughing at my conversation with the universe that ensued. And the other bathrobe hanging there had just a normal label of some company.*

I never did find out the real story of this robe that had "VER-MONT" on its label. I asked at the front desk as we were leaving the next morning, and the clerk said, "Are you sure it didn't say 'Velours'?"

But the message I heard from the universe when I read that label went something like this: "Hello, Susan; you made it! You think you don't know where you are going, but you do. You are right on course and exactly where you are supposed to be. Keep listening, keep paying attention, one foot in front of the other, as you continue on your path. There will be more clues along the way. Love, The Universe (AKA The Mystery That Loves You)."

I have been wearing a pendant for about a year now—a gold swan on a chain (an eBay purchase, I confess). I liked the symbolism when I looked up "swan" in that book I've mentioned before by Ted Andrews, Animal Speak. *The keynote for swan is "awakening the true beauty and power of the Self." After my trip to Ireland, I was rummaging around looking for something in my jewelry box and came across a small Celtic cross that I had never worn. It occurred to me to hang the cross and the swan together on a chain, and as soon as I looked in the mirror, I was instantly transported back to Ireland, in particular to St. Stephen's Green in Dublin. By chance I had arrived there early in the morning, on our only day in Dublin, and was able to see the caretaker feeding the swans their breakfast. I think most of my bus companions were still in bed. It felt like a private viewing, and I very much felt Dan's presence there with me in that park. It seemed a happy place—full of beautiful old trees, pathways, and sculptures honoring historical figures, including famous writers and poets.*

And then, putting on the necklace with the swan and cross, I saw further meaning. When I look at the cross, I am reminded of great suffering—and mercy, too. I think of Jesus' suffering on the cross, of course, but I also think of Dan's suffering, especially the very last week of his life. And our family and Natalie's suffering at Dan's dying. But with the swan there, I am reminded that one cannot contemplate death without also including resurrection and new life. Each ending is also a new beginning. I like to believe that Dan's dying has helped—and continues to help—"awaken the true beauty and power of the Self," because it is since Dan's dying that I have felt myself returning to myself.

I don't really have the right words to express this, but perhaps you will understand anyway. Long-forgotten memories have surfaced—images, feelings—as though Dan's dying blasted away a boulder and, as a result, more that was hidden is now released and able to surface to become integrated into who I am. Maybe this just naturally happens in the aging process, but I like to thank Dan for perhaps speeding this transformation along.

In reading just now (Dec. 29) about the Celtic cross (and they were everywhere we traveled in Ireland), it says that the joining part, where the vertical meets the horizontal, represents the unification of heaven and earth. The number four holds great meaning. The circle portion symbolizes eternal life and God's infinite Love. It also represents wholeness and completion. I like to think of the cross with the swan as suffering transformed into beauty and wholeness.

A few days ago I found myself coming home with an unexpected purchase. Again, I don't really know how it happened, but I was somehow led to buy an unframed wood-block print made by a local artist. It is of a sparrow surrounded by wild branches with light behind it. When I got home, being curious, I looked up "sparrow" in Animal Speak. Among other things, it said that the sparrow was "the one bird present throughout the crucifixion of Christ, making it a symbol of triumph after long suffering." It also said, "The sparrow will awaken within you a new sense of dignity and self-worth, helping you to triumph in spite of outer circumstances." I think this is a perfect present to honor the fifth anniversary of Dan's passing.

This evening (Dec. 26), we are picking Natalie up at the train station, and tomorrow I will take her to the airport—Natalie is going to Uganda for about three weeks. A few weeks ago she graduated from a very difficult, intense, three-year graduate program at the University of Vermont and is now a nurse practitioner. Gregg and I attended her graduation, which was very moving for me on many levels—not the least of which was that I knew, beyond a shadow of a doubt, that Dan was there. We could not be more proud of her. In Uganda she will assist with teaching a class offered to senior UVM nursing students studying and working in healthcare in Uganda. She says it was Dan who encouraged her to apply for the nurse practitioner degree. And most assuredly, Dan has been helping her, especially when things were difficult with a professor who was most challenging.

Andy and family are well! His children (my grandchildren) are now ages ten, eight, and four. I will be visiting them for a few days in January.

Gregg is getting ready to retire in May. I just work for a few hours now and then at the Co-op. We are on the cusp of change and a new chapter in our marriage. I am so glad to be alive at this stage of life. In O'Donohue's book (the full title is Anam Cara: A Book of Celtic Wisdom*), he speaks of this season in one's life as the time of "inner harvesting." I love this wording. He writes, "Inner harvesting means that you actually begin to sift the fruits of your experience. You begin to group, select, and integrate them." He also writes:*

> *Old age, as the harvest of life, is a time when your times and their fragments gather. In this way, you unify yourself and achieve a new strength, poise, and belonging that was never available to you when you were distractedly rushing through your days. Old age is a time of coming home to your deeper nature, of entering fully into the temple of your mem-*

ory where all your vanished days are secretly gathered and awaiting you.

I feel so blessed and rich beyond words, most especially because I have time. Time to be quiet and listen for the messages Mystery is sending my way. Time to be in holy presence with friends. I know that horrific things are happening in the world, all the time— things so unimaginably abhorrent that we cannot fully wrap our brains around them. And yet I choose to believe in Love—that Love is the larger circle containing it all, that Love is the ultimate and lasting truth.

I know for some of you this has been a very difficult year. Please know that our door is open to you, the guest bed is made, and the teakettle is just minutes away from boiling. Nothing would give me more pleasure than to see you on my doorstep.

I notice from my past letters that I often like to include a poem. I'll leave you with this one from Anam Cara.

Much love to you all,
Susan/Susie/Sue

A Blessing of Solitude

May you recognize in your life the presence, power, and light
   of your soul.
May you realize that you are never alone,
that your soul in its brightness and belonging connects you
   intimately with the rhythm of the universe.
May you have respect for your own individuality and
   difference.

May you realize that the shape of your soul is unique, that
  you have a special destiny here,
that behind the façade of your life there is something
  beautiful, good, and eternal happening.
May you learn to see yourself with the same delight, pride,
  and expectation with which God sees you in every moment.

I HAVE ALWAYS thought of myself as being more of a dancer
than a singer. Seated in an audience listening to music, I am
sometimes startled to see that almost everyone is sitting there
completely still, while I am usually swaying, or moving my hands
or feet or some other body part. I can't help it. Music calls to me
to move to it.

I have a memory of dancing when I was little. A classical record
is playing in the house. There may have been others around, but
I am caught up in my own world, twirling and swooping, I move
from room to room as I try to express the story I imagine the
music is telling. A number of years ago, I used to occasionally
attend a full-moon dancing gathering. It was held in a beautiful space, a small building with a dome skylight in the middle
of the roof and polished hardwood floors. We were led in folk
dances. With joined hands, we circled around candles placed in
the center of the floor. Smaller candles in window alcoves cast
flickering shadows on the warm peach-colored walls. It was quite
magical. I usually caught on pretty quickly to the dances; it was
not a mental kind of thing, more a matter of getting out of my
head and just letting my body do what it knew how to do. One
night in particular, it might have been a Greek dance we were
learning, and I had the thought that I must have danced that one
in a past life because it seemed some part of me already knew
the dance. There are many ways to pray, and I was definitely one

who liked to "sweat [my] prayers" (a term coined by Gabrielle Roth).

But there seems to be less opportunity for movement in this day and age, and more for singing. Maybe because singing takes up less room! I grew up having been told, and believing, that I didn't have much of a singing voice. Nonetheless, I was invited to participate in a most welcoming Unitarian-Universalist choir. Over time, I found I wasn't such a bad singer after all.

My second year singing with the choir, some of us attended an annual event called "The Great Day of Singing." Singers from far and wide would meet on a Saturday afternoon at a designated church in a city in Vermont and learn songs from other choir directors. I really don't read music, or barely, so it was definitely challenging. I was quite enjoying myself when something came along that completely caught me off-guard. We had barely started into a new song when I was just overcome. I had the sense that angels had flown into our presence. Dan was there too. The music was beyond beautiful. My eyes filled with tears and I could not sing because the emotion was so great. I felt totally connected to the sacred and the holy.

I felt in a somewhat altered state for the rest of the day, and the next day, too. I Googled the song and listened to it many times. The song is called "Requiem," by Eliza Gilkyson. She had written it as a song of comfort, a song of grief in response to the Asian tsunami of 2004. I do believe artists are often inspired by a Source beyond their knowing, and I feel it to be true with this particular song, that it was a gift given to the composer to bring comfort to this world. It speaks of a tenderness, a compassion, deeper than we can fathom.

That Sunday night, before going to sleep, I was in between the fiction books I usually read and reached instead for a book of poetry, thinking I would just read one or two before turning out the light. This particular book of poems, *New and Selected Poems,* by Mary Oliver, is one I once loaned to Dan, and he had drawn and written on some of the poems. I opened at random to a poem near the end of the book called "Clam Man." And there, although there is nothing in the poem to do with music, what I saw and had never noticed before was that Dan had written at the bottom in large capital letters:

"SING!"

So somewhere along the journey, I have moved from a sweat-your-prayers kind of a person to a sing-your-prayers being. I sing now in the community chorus where roughly 100 singers young and old join voices to sing songs of comfort, gratitude, and praise. And every now and then, I am blessed to sing a song like the aforementioned "Requiem" or one called "Luminous Night of the Soul," by Ola Gjeilo. Then the veil becomes thin and I feel transported. Dan seems so near and I catch just a glimpse of the numinous world that I imagine he now calls home.

2014 (email)

Dear Friends,

I have debated whether to bother telling you this or wait until my next letter, although I don't know if there will even be a next letter, or if it might not be until another year...but this "coincidence" just seems too extraordinary to pass up. In fact, so extraordinary that I have trouble even calling it a coincidence.

To backtrack a little, when Dan's cancer came back in 2008 (or maybe it had never left), he, Gregg, and Natalie drove back down to Mass General to meet with a top-notch oncologist (a sarcoma expert). It was after that meeting that Dan and Nat decided to transfer Dan's case to Dana Farber, where he pursued some clinical trials.

When Natalie was in Uganda as a TA in January, she worked with about 10 UVM nursing students. They all got along great. It was an absolutely amazing trip, including a safari at the end where Nat saw giraffes, hippos, monkeys, elephants, lions, alligators, deer, and more. And it was on that trip, walking by a little outdoor market, that Natalie saw a Willamette sweatshirt hanging up! Most people haven't even heard of this small university that Dan attended in Oregon. But here was this Willamette sweatshirt in Uganda, of all places. Later that day, her friends bought it for Natalie as a surprise.

Anyway, one of the students went by the name Collier, though her given name was Eliza. Nat didn't know the last names of most of the students. It was only after she got back to Vermont that she learned of Collier's last name and that her dad was an oncologist at Mass General. And indeed, her dad was the very doctor Dan had worked with!

I find the likelihood of all this quite amazing. Mass General is a huge place, with many oncologists. This particular doctor's daughter could have gone to school anywhere, and then for her and Natalie to end up on this trip together in Uganda? As I say, for me, it is beyond coincidence. More like part of some intended grand plan.

Meanwhile, Natalie has always said she wanted to do something to raise sarcoma awareness. After discovering the connection, she mentioned this to Collier, who of course got in touch with her dad. He remembered Dan, sent his condolences and also mentioned there is a walk in May that raises money for sarcoma research. Nat is hoping to participate this year.

I tell you all this because there is so much out there that we will never know or understand. But at times, there does seem to be some sort of a divine plan at work, don't you think? The way one *life touches another, an unfolding that is a beautiful mystery to behold.*

Thanks for listening!

xxx,

Me

THE ANNUAL 12,402 Steps to Cure Sarcoma Walk 2014 was held in Hudson, Massachusetts, on a beautiful Saturday in mid-May, roughly five years after Dan's dying. Gregg and I arrived the evening before and enjoyed a lovely dinner out with Natalie and her parents, who were staying at the same hotel as us, on the same floor. One of Natalie's friends from Middlebury College had recently become a doctor. She lives and works in Massachusetts and joined us for the Walk.

The most significant image I carry with me from that day is walking slightly behind Natalie at one point. I got to quietly observe her as she chatted with her walking companions, who at that moment were none other than Dan's former oncologist and his daughter who had been with Natalie in Uganda. This dedicated doctor is one of the organizers of the fundraiser. Before the actual walking started, he spoke to the huge crowd about the history and the importance of the Jennifer Hunter Yates Sarcoma Foundation, and of the many ways the Foundation supports sarcoma research and the patients and families of those with sarcoma cancer. We all wore special t-shirts handed out when we registered. The cancer survivors wore differently colored shirts from ours and walked at the head of the march.

Watching Natalie as she walked and talked, I had the sense of a circle being closed. A loose end being tied in order to make something right. A healing of sorts. Dan had left Mass General somewhat abruptly. Now, here was Natalie, and the doctor and his daughter, caring for each other and united in their desire to help find a cure for sarcoma. Something unfinished had transformed into a completion that was beautiful and meaningful.

Originally, Natalie set a fundraising goal of $500. Given all of my wonderful friends who had supported Dan and Natalie in their journey, I knew her goal was much too modest. We could do a lot better than that!

The Walk raised over $90,000 that day. Natalie and her donors, whom we called "Team Dan," raised over $3,700! In fact, I think hers was one of the highest-grossing individual teams. Natalie was thrilled, and Dan's former oncologist was quite taken aback. Apparently the teams that raise the most are usually locally based, near to Boston. I told him, "Well, there's a lot of love in Vermont!"

April 14, 2014 (email)

For those of you who like short emails, stop here and push delete! Natalie just called—she passed her exam and is now officially a board certified nurse practitioner! She says all the good thoughts and energy sent her way really helped. She thanks you all, as do I. So much.

I happened to have time to myself this morning and decided I might write a poem while Natalie was taking her exam. It was a poem I had anticipated being able to write over the weekend, but that never happened. Yesterday a title popped into my head, "The Poem I Didn't Write." Today I wrote it.

Just a little context for you. Seven years ago this July, I had an impromptu healing circle at our house the day before Dan's leg amputation at Mass General. Many of you were there. I led everyone around the yard, and we would stop here and there to say something, or read something, before continuing to wind our

*way to the next stopping point. I had been given a poem shortly
before that day, and I read it at that circle. It's called "Kindness,"
by Naomi Shihab Nye. (I included it with the first letter.)*

*This weekend there was a conference in Burlington called "The
Full Circle" conference, where the theme was women and aging.
And the guest speaker was none other than Naomi Shihab Nye!
My friend did not know about the healing circle seven years ago
and the importance of that poem in my life, but she thought I
really needed to attend the writing workshop. Although we were
wait-listed, we did end up getting into it, and that is where I
thought I might write a poem.*

*But it was not meant to be. Others in the workshop wrote
amazing things, in such a short period of time, but I was not one
of them. Nor did I take the time to tell Naomi about her poem
and Dan, and how "full circle" had a special meaning for me. But
this morning I wrote it! (I guess you never know when inspiration
will strike.) My poem will probably be edited over time but here is
today's copy. Thanks for letting me share it.*

S.

*P.S. Interestingly, Naomi told us she wrote the poem "Kindness"
while in Colombia (Natalie is half Colombian) after she and her
husband had all their belongings stolen. What is interesting to me
is that she said this poem is different from most of hers because it
was one that seemed to just come to her. She just copied it down
as it came, which is not usually how she writes. This feels true
to me, because I sense her poem is tapping into something much
deeper than the sudden loss of one's luggage, belongings, or whatever. It was a gift to her, to share with the world.*

Here is my poem:

The Poem I Didn't Write

By Susan Humphrey
(dedicated to Naomi Shihab Nye, who wrote "Kindness,"
and to Natalie Anne Guarin on the day of her becoming
a board certified Nurse Practitioner)

How could I tell you
In one short poem, the full
Circle of then and now,
From your poem "Kindness"
To my being here today
And whole.
So much more of me now
Than seven years ago when
We circled around, in and out,
The sun warm on our backs.
Birds calling
We snaked through the yard,
Hand in hand,
Past garden stones and swing set
Where my children
had played.
A healing circle of women we felt
The enormity of threshold,
Holy spirit, blessed life,
We stopped under the pin oak.
We read "Kindness" not knowing
What lay ahead.
Held in presence with those
Seen and Unseen, Known and Unknown,
The leaves fluttered—it was hot

In July, but not unbearably so.
I gathered the end of the
Orange cloth and wove in and
Out of our circle, pulling us
Up into a braid of caring—
Such love! Not knowing then
Dan would die, yet
Life would not stop,
At times painfully so,
Life would not stop.
Then Kindness, like you wrote,
Became the only thing that
Made sense anymore. And Natalie,
Healing, became a Nurse Practitioner.
We are older now, fuller,
Dan and Kindness have twined
Into One,
Palpable teacher, willing friend,
Mirror of our best selves,
My son.

December 2014–January 2015

Dear Friends,

"My house is full of stories" is a phrase that popped into my head quite a few years ago. I always thought it would be a wonderful title for a book of poetry or perhaps short stories. It is a title waiting for its book.

I think of so many things to tell you in and out of a year. It is hard choosing. I know the silences are as important as what is said, the space in between the lines as important as the lines themselves.

I will write you of some of the threads of my life, always tipping my hat of gratitude to Dan, who continues to be ever present in one way or another, now coming up to the sixth anniversary of his dying. I do feel the stories in my house almost as a living presence. Some go back very far, before I was even born. I moved every four years of my life before arriving here, in 1978, at our dear 402 Thompson Hill Road, Weybridge, Vermont. Home.

This year, more than any other in my memory, I find myself especially appreciative of place and being surrounded by stories inside and out. They ground and shape me. And I am grateful to people who have come recently into my life to help with home repairs, landscaping, etc. Their humor, quirkiness, artistry, and expertise are part of what makes the home landscape so beautiful to me.

Dan C. came to clear brush. I quickly learned to make myself absent, at least part of the time, or he would truly talk my ear off with stories that you think are probably true, but you're never quite sure. He knows about trees and wild animals and nature and all sorts of other stuff, too. Best of all, he's not allergic or afraid of poison ivy, and he and our dog, Buddy, really hit it off, too. I liked Dan immediately just because of his name. Have you ever met a Dan you didn't like?

Then there's Bernie. Bernie made us a wrought-iron railing for the front steps. He grew up in East Germany but always dreamed of coming to this country. And when the wall came down, he did. He arrived in New York City young and strong, but with little money to his name, not knowing a soul and speaking no English! His stories of the kindness of strangers who took him in, and his adventures working across this country and finally settling in Ben-son, Vermont, are ones I hope I never forget. I often hold on to the railing he made, even when it's not slippery, just to be reminded of Bernie and the resilience of the human spirit.

Sam brought me a new apple tree. Years ago, Sam's mother,

Connie, whom I hardly knew, invited us to stay a few days in her summer home in Maine when we wanted to visit Andy, who was working for a family nearby. I brought a coffee table book on flowers to give as a thank you present. On the cover of this book was a striking illustration of a bouquet of flowers.

Shortly after arriving at Connie's house, I walked into a living room in the back of the house and there was a bouquet of flowers in a glass vase on a table. I stopped dead in my tracks because, as far as I was concerned, the bouquet of flowers on the table was none other than the one on the cover of the book I'd brought. They were that similar. Later on, when no one was looking, I even took a photo of the vase of flowers next to the book. It is hard to put into words the feeling I had. I think it was very similar to the one I wrote about last year: When in Ireland staying one night in a castle, I lifted the collar of a bathrobe hanging in the elegant bathroom to find that the label said "Vermont." The feeling for both of these experiences I might say was one of "recognition." But recognition of exactly what, I cannot say!

Anyway—back to Maine and Connie's house. All of this happened long before Connie would die of cancer, and Dan too, and Sam would become a landscape designer in Maine and eventually move back with his family to Vermont, where in the fall of 2014 he would come to help me with my gardens.

Sam is the one who suggested planting the crabapple at the front of the house—Malus "Bob White" is its proper name. At the last minute I started getting cold feet; I wasn't sure it was the right choice and I hadn't actually seen it. But I was too late in reaching Sam, and he arrived in his pick-up truck with this fairly good-sized tree sticking out the back. I spoke to him of my doubts, but Sam calmly said, "It will be beautiful and you will love it." I just let go of my fears and trusted him. And he was right! In early December in the process of stringing strands of little white lights, which involved climbing up on a ladder to get to some of the *higher branches, I became quite bonded with the tree and started calling him "Bob." Turning his lights on each evening is now one of my favorite daily rituals through this dark wintry time.*

Like a title waiting for its book, there is a small wrought-iron chair in my garage waiting for its garden! I'd admired it a few years ago at a friend's house. She'd gotten it for very little at a second-hand shop but decided it just wasn't what she wanted after all, and so she passed it on to me, not even knowing that I'd started dreaming up a new garden space. The chair has the shape of a fern in its backrest and I am planning to put it in a shade garden I hope to create—and to call the garden "Fernglade."

I am thinking this garden could be dedicated to the memory of our furry friends, and especially to our dog, Buddy, whom we put down in November after a long and joy-filled life. Buddy loved running around back there, near the brook, while Dan C. cleared the bushes and poison ivy and where, hopefully, a garden will grow.

I see I have gone in a bit of a circle—which brings me back to asking you what brings you joy. For me, lots of things, but this year I believe I have felt my most contented self while planning and caring for the land I live on. It does not feel like a selfish endeavor somehow, but as though I am working for, and with, something much larger than myself—and for the benefit of others, not just my own personal pleasure. A phrase that popped into my head one day while I was engaged in this work was "Make a garden of your grief." I really like this thought, both literally and metaphorically. For indeed, there is incredible, transformative power in one's grief.

Last winter, maybe in February, I was sorting through piles of papers when I came across a page where I had written down something Dan had said. I don't keep a diary, but I occasionally write things down that seem important. It was lovely to come upon this, dated "12/18," but no year was given. It seems Dan must have been in college. What I wrote was, "Dan home. Says he doesn't need anything for Xmas and hopes we didn't buy him much. He says we're so fortunate to have this house. He keeps saying our house is amazing, and the land too. Even most millionaires don't have what we have."

So maybe when I am working on the land and taking care of our house (which I consider nice, but modest), I am also feeling Dan's blessing. I like to imagine I hear his voice saying, "Good work, Mom."

I cannot write about the joys without also including the sorrows. What makes you sad and/or anxious? There are any number of reasons to find oneself feeling appalled, shaken or just terribly, terribly sad. The strangest thing for me is that sometimes I just feel these feelings in my body for no apparent reason. At these times I usually wonder what story I am holding in my body. What is this dread? I don't have any special technique for getting through difficult feelings—do you? I think I usually wait them out, sit with them, move with them. Sometimes I simply say, "Thank you." There is something about that simple statement…it seems to help things move along positively once again.

*When Sam suggested I might put some apple trees along the driveway going up to the house, I immediately recognized this thought as my own. I, too, had had this vision before, only the timing wasn't right. And then I remembered one of my favorite picture books as a child—*The Little House, *by Virginia Lee Burton, who also wrote* Mike Mulligan and His Steam Shovel. *In this story, the little house lived on a hill, surrounded by apple trees. She was well-loved and happy but then went through a period of being forgotten and falling into disrepair. She was very, very sad. But in the end she was rediscovered—in a sense brought back to life—and loved once again.*

I see this story now as one of transformation, of waiting patiently, of family bonds threading through generations, and

ultimately of the redeeming power of love to heal and to restore
oneself to oneself. Sam had not heard of this book, though I felt
sure it was most likely one his mother had read to him. I gave him
a paperback copy to keep, to read to his own children. I imagined
Connie smiling.

Gregg, Andy and family, Natalie all are well, and I hope your
loved ones are too.

I wish you the best of stories for 2015. May they heal and nour-
ish you through all the seasons, through all sorts of weather!

Much love,
Susan, Susie, Sue

I HAVE MENTIONED OUR DOG, Buddy, in several letters. Everyone who met Buddy, a medium-sized beagle/shepherd mix,
loved him. He was a therapy dog by nature. In the weeks before
Dan died, he was often with us at Dan and Natalie's apartment in
town. After Dan died Natalie was always happy to see us, but I
knew she was just as eager to spend some time with Buddy.

We never knew exactly how old Buddy was, as he had shown
up at our house back in July 2005. On a Friday morning I was at
a friend's house participating in a writing exercise known as pro-
prioceptive writing, a method of exploring the mind and heart
through writing. That morning, when my friend's dog walked by,
I started writing about my fantasy of someday having a dog again.
We had put down our dear old Bassett hound, Merlin, about nine
months prior. In my writing I wondered about what kind of a
dog I might like, and how I'd probably have to wait until I was
working less. I ended by writing, "Knowing me, I'll never be able
to decide. So some sweet animal will just have to fall into my lap
when the time is right."

Three days later Buddy showed up. We live in the country at

the end of a fairly long driveway. There are other houses closer to the road, but Buddy walked up to ours. He had no collar and seemed in a great mood. He was smiling.

I called neighbors and all of the appropriate organizations to try to find his owner. By the end of the first day (by the end of the first few hours!), I knew that Buddy was the dog I had been writing about, and that if no one claimed him, we would adopt him. No one did call, and Buddy became a wonderful part of our family. Even the cats who joined our family towards the end of his life adored him.

I won't go into all the details of his life, but by the time he was nearing the end, I was working less and could spend more time with him. In fact, I am guessing that the last few months of his life were some of his best. He had kidney disease, and I told him he was in hospice care now, which meant it was all about quality of life for however much time remained.

He got to go outside whenever he wanted. Because of his kidneys, he often didn't feel like eating. We were constantly trying to entice him with various yummy dishes. He dined on roast chicken, poached salmon, and chicken pot pies from the grocery store, leftover spaghetti, stir-fry, or whatever we were eating. And on one particular afternoon, after a morning when he chased a squirrel and ate a delicious breakfast and lunch, he was suddenly in terrible pain. The pain did not last long because we were able to get him to the vet fairly quickly. We knew it was his time. With gentleness and respect, the vet first sedated him and then put him down. I, of course, spoke to Dan and asked him, if he could, to please be there to greet Buddy on the Other Side.

One reason I am telling you this story is because Dan and Buddy are the only two important beings in my life about whom I have had a vivid dream after their deaths. I mentioned earlier the dream about Dan, when he came to me as a little boy, when he put his hand in mine and I could truly *feel* it.

I don't remember how long it was after Buddy's death that I dreamt of him. Interestingly, I was napping on the same couch where I'd dreamt of Dan. But in this dream, it was even more real, because I was lying on that couch in the dream itself. Buddy came right up to my face. I could smell him and hear his breathing. I remember thinking how I'd forgotten how he smelled and how it sounded when he licked his chops of extra saliva. I could see him too, even with my eyes closed. I knew he was supposed to be dead. But I was 99 percent sure he was really there and that there was even a good explanation of how this could be possible. Like a new way of understanding reality. I think it occurred to me there was a possibility that if I opened my eyes he would not be there anymore. But more of me believed he truly was there, and that I would see him with open eyes. So with great effort I forced my eyelids open. Buddy was gone.

I still wonder about both of these vivid dreams. I still wonder if there could be alternate realities out there that we have yet to understand.

November–December 2015

Dear Friends,

A letter has been brewing in my head for several weeks now. Have you felt me reaching out to you? It seems to happen most often while I'm driving in the car, which is really annoying since I can't write down what is coming up!

Today the thought that came to me is that my life feels a bit like a really good book! If one can just live long enough, like into one's sixties, then one can start to see the pieces fall into place: how seemingly random events at the time of their happening are really not so random after all but part of a beautiful design—a beauty no less rich than an exquisite oriental rug or a book with many twists, turns and subplots that somehow become all connected and part of the whole by the last page.

And then there's the phrase "curiouser and curiouser" that I found myself whispering one day. Where did that come from? It's from Alice in Wonderland and must have been lying in my subconscious all these many years now, as I did play Alice in our senior high school play. The curious thing about that was that I don't recall trying out for the part. But I did like acting in those days, and I did wear my hair much like Alice, down and held back on occasion by a simple headband or ribbon. I probably uttered that line in 1970, having no idea that life would indeed, become curiouser and curiouser....

In September I went to put on my necklace, the one with the small Celtic cross and gold swan that I wrote you about after my trip to Ireland. I had not been wearing it over the summer because it was so hot out. I could not find it anywhere. I know this is a minor event in the grand scheme of things, but it felt big. Not so much the actual loss of the necklace, but more that I had been unaware it was missing. My brain felt very odd indeed; I was grateful I didn't have to make any important decisions that day. It was as though something had suddenly changed, a brain wire shift. As Alice said, "I knew who I was this morning, but I've changed a few times since then."

Once I came back to feeling more grounded, I decided that whether that necklace ever showed up again or not, the universe was telling me that life was flowing on, and like it or not, it was time to find another necklace that would have special meaning for who I am now. I'll continue the thread of this particular story later on in the letter.

"Dan Moments" continue to occur in our lives, and I experienced a particularly strong one in August. We had attended a celebratory dinner in New London, CT, where Natalie and fellow

N.P.s graduated from a year-long residency program, the oldest such program in the country. Of course we felt Dan there because whenever I'm with Natalie, I feel Dan's presence more strongly. But Nat's Dad even mentioned Dan, and how important he was in helping her decide to become a nurse practitioner in the first place. The next day, I was home alone downloading onto my computer all the photos I'd taken from the dinner. I will say that I was in a wistful, longing mood. I was missing Dan; I was missing Natalie. At one point, my computer said there was an error in the download process. But when I went to import them again, I saw that all the photos had indeed been imported successfully.

However, instead of showing an image in my photo library, there was just a blank gray square. If one clicked on it, it brought up other blank squares, and if one clicked on those, one could see all the photos from the dinner. As I scrolled down these blank-looking squares to get to one near the end, all the squares suddenly lit up with a photograph. How curious! This lasted less than a second, so at first I really could not see what it was showing. I had to keep scrolling to get the image to pop up. Finally I recognized it. And I was shocked to see it was the last photo I took of Dan, likely the day before he died.

I know there is some rational reason that would explain how a photograph buried in files from 2009 could suddenly show up in this current file, basically on top of other photographs. But because of the timing and the particular mood I was in, my heart so filled with Dan and Nat that I felt sure he was there—that he was reaching out to me. I imagined he was saying, "Well done, Natalie!" (for completing the residency) and that he was reminding me, once again, that though we can't see him, at certain times like significant occasions, he is ever near, just behind the veil.

Last year I wrote you about our newly landscaped front yard and the pleasure of playing in the soil. Pleasure, but also work. In fact at one point late in the summer, I decided I'd taken on a new *part-time job—watering! We went weeks with very little rain, and I spent hours each morning, or so it seemed, watering all those new plantings. I have friends who meditate each day; I decided this watering routine was my new practice, my own form of meditation. The heat and drought seemed unrelenting. One morning I heard myself thinking, "I'm not sure I can last until the next rain; I'm not sure my plants can last." Not long after that I noticed our bird bath, which sits on the ground, was starting to be blocked by some plantings. I moved it forward to give it a little more room and then I got the idea of floating some flowers in it. I picked a few impatiens nearby and arranged them on the surface of the water. And then somehow, the bird bath just took on the look of an offering to the Gods (in hope of rain!). And then it dawned on me what I'd done, and I almost laughed out loud at the irony of it all. Floating impatiens, of all things. I could practically hear the universe laughing back. I was offering up my impatiens and it was saying, "Yes, Susan, you need to be more patient!"*

The next day Gregg and I both saw a bird in the bird bath, and we'd never seen one there before (mostly it had been our dog's outdoor watering dish). So I felt my offering was received. And not too many days later, we did get a sprinkle of rain, though it would be a good week or more before we'd get the huge downpour we really needed and had been waiting for. And speaking of patience, here is a gardening quote that showed up on my computer screen last April when I was looking up information on the shrub fothergilla (don't you love that name?). I'd forgotten all about it until I saw it yesterday in a book where I write down good quotes that find me.

Everything that slows us down and forces patience, everything that sets us back into the slow circle of nature, is a help. Gardening is an instrument of grace.

—May Sarton, Journal of a Solitude

Okay, back to the story of a lost necklace, a mini identity crisis, and the search for a new talisman. I quickly looked on eBay where I'd purchased the little cross and the swan in the first place. Could I just replace them? I did find the Celtic cross still available on the site of the maker. But the swan was a piece I would likely never find again. Just as well, I supposed—as Alice said, "I can't go back to yesterday because I was a different person then." Ever onward. I looked at several charms on eBay, animals and birds, hoping one would call out to me (and be affordable!). I kept coming back to one listed as a "descending dove." But the seller did not offer returns, which made me hesitant. But after a nice email from the seller, I took the chance. I remember well the afternoon I hit "Buy it Now," because it was the very day of the huge downpour we'd all (gardeners, that is) been waiting for. It rained hard all day, and we got about 3½ inches, as I recall.

The next day, when I happened to look up "dove" in that book I love, Animal Speak, I felt pretty certain I'd bought the right charm/pendant. It even mentioned rain, the word most on my mind in recent weeks. Among other things it says, "The voice of the dove is the rain song. Out of its mourning, it invokes new waters of life...the song of this totem tells you to mourn what has passed but awaken to the promise of the future. It is a bird of prophecy and can help you to see what you can give birth to in your life." And of course, in Christian lore, the dove represents the Holy Spirit and the heavenly messenger.

We are climbing now, in this letter. I am trying to get us to the mountains of Montserrat, Spain, but we are not quite there yet! Over three years ago, Gregg and I paid for a travel opportunity we felt was just too good to pass up. Although it was a cruise (and we did not consider ourselves to be "cruise" people), it was stopping at many ports in places we both had been intrigued to see. Telling you about this trip, which we took in October, could be a letter in itself; maybe another time. For now, what I will tell you is that it was a whirlwind—so many places in just two weeks.

It felt quite surreal to be on a Mediterranean cruise, and I had to pinch myself a few times. We started in the magical city of Venice (where it was raining, no less) and ended in Barcelona, with eight stops in between. One of the first paintings I saw in Venice, at the Accademia, was a beautiful rendition in rich blues, reds, and gold of the angel coming to Mary. And in the middle, above Mary's halo, was a descending dove, reminding me of my necklace. I decided right then and there that the dove would be my north star on this trip—that wherever we went, I would look for it. And when I would see it, I would pause, take a deep breath, and know all was well. It was my little secret. I did not tell Gregg about this, and I spotted that dove everywhere we went, from start to finish. At our last destination, Barcelona, Gregg chose a tour to view the incredible work of the renowned architect Gaudi, while I chose to make a pilgrimage to an ancient Benedictine monastery in Montserrat, home to a renowned and beloved Black Madonna, also known as La Moreneta. I stood close to the front of the packed basilica, near a large stained glass window (whose scene included a descending dove). From there I had a clear, though distant, view of the Black Madonna, and I could watch and hear the famous boys' choir sing praises with their sweet angelic voices. Later I lit a candle for Dan and Natalie, and placed it among hundreds of others along the Ave Maria path (cami del'Ave Maria).

Although I had seen so many images on this trip of a crucified Jesus (including Michelangelo's Pieta in St. Peter's Basilica in Vatican City), probably the most moving one of all was a painting in a side chapel off of the Basilica in Montserrat. It showed Mary holding Jesus, but instead of looking down at him, she was looking up. And what catches you by surprise is, the face of this Mary looks modern-day. Suddenly, she is not so much Mary, Mother of Jesus, she is simply a mother, holding her dead son. She is one of us, and the darkish landscape in the background so well captures the bleak territory of grief that one must cross through to get to the other side.

I experienced Montserrat as a holy site; the energies of hopeful prayers, of pain, suffering, and compassion were quite palpable. People go there to pray for miracles, and at the very least they receive unconditional, healing love. I felt privileged, and very moved, to be there.

I love that I had one last Dan moment at the end of the trip in Barcelona, just before getting on the bus to head back to the ship. We were walking to the bus and passed a group of street musicians whose music was joyful and contagious. I was drawn to it like a bee to honey. I especially could not take my eyes off one of the lead singers in the middle because he was playing a saxophone (one of Dan's favored instruments), as well as maracas. The music was so infectious, I knew Dan would have loved it. I could feel him there with me. In fact, I half expected to see him slip into the group with saxophone in hand to start jamming with them. It is such a sweet and happy image for me to have on this last day of an otherworldly journey.

And back on the ship, later that evening (our last on board), I suddenly flashed on another dove. Maybe my memory was jogged because, although he was not born there, Barcelona is considered by many to be the home of Picasso. And in Dan and Nat's apartment, there was a poster on a wall above the keyboard where Dan played. It was a poster of a Picasso dove with words by Pablo Neruda underneath. The words were "Mi deber es vivir, moirir, vivir." (My duty is to live, to die, to live.)

Dear ones, we are coming to the end of this particular journey (which, of course, is just another beginning). I have been writing some of you since 2007, while others of you have become my friends along the way. I can't thank you enough for your generous listening, for really taking this writing journey right alongside me. Some of you have encouraged me to try to put my letters together in a book that could perhaps have a wider audience. And I may try to do that in the next year (with significant editing).

It has been eight years since I started writing to you, and seven since Dan died. My youngest grandchild, Hadley, was in her mommy's tummy when Dan died, and now she is 6 years old! Drew and Phoebe are 12 and 10 years old, respectively. I do not see them as often as I would like, but I feel great joy and gratitude that they are well and happy (as are Andy and his wife, Megan).

We gave Drew one of Dan's saxophones this year, the alto sax, and he is learning to play it at school in band. And each year, in May, I pass out the annual Dan Humphrey Music Scholarship to a deserving student in the high school jazz band. I always feel Dan with me on that occasion.

I came across a poem this year that seems fitting for me to share here. It says so much in just a few words:

Separation

Your absence has gone through me
like thread through a needle.
Everything I do is stitched with its color.

—W. S. Merwin

And what became of that new necklace, you ask?

"Who in the world am I?" asks Alice. "Ah, that's the great puzzle!" Isn't it fantastic that we can work on that puzzle for all of our lives? Wearing my new necklace is both a comfort and a challenge. It seems to invite me to live more deeply, to keep growing in wisdom and compassion. It was starting to feel a little "heavy," until one day I happened to look down. The chain is long enough that I can

see it from this upside down vantage point, and what I saw was not a dove, but a dolphin. And it made me laugh because I immediately thought "playful"!

So while the dove speaks of spirit, compassion and new life, the dolphin reminds me not to take myself too seriously and to be playful. As Gandhi once said, "Service which is rendered without joy helps neither the servant nor the served." I ask myself these days, how am I being called to serve, now, at this particular time in my life? Dolphin reminds me to be sure to include playfulness and joy in that recipe of service.

The gold charm has one more level worth mentioning. Sometimes, it looks to me oddly familiar, like a letter from an ancient alphabet. This speaks to me of my unknown past (I'm half Jewish)—of my ancestors and even past lives—all that has brought me to this current incarnation. I am content leaving that mystery as something I will likely never fully know or understand. But I can give profound thanks for its presence in my life.

I have traced the pendant to show you the dove and the upside down view, the dolphin.

These are troubling times in much of the world. I have no answers or even suggestions. But surely friendship and hospitality are two of the greatest gifts we can share. May it be so.

Blessings to you all,
Susan/Susie/Sue

P.S. November 28 was our 40th wedding anniversary. Natalie did not know this, nor did she know about my dove connection. But *on that day she emailed us that, by chance (ha!), as she was catching up on chart notes, a beautiful song had come on her Brubeck Pandora station. Dan loved Brubeck, and she thought he would have loved this song. Maybe he knew it. She said it's called "La Paloma Azul"—The Blue Dove.*

Excerpt from email sent May 2016:

After Dan died we set up the Dan Humphrey Music Scholarship. Each year we award an MUHS jazz band student a small stipend to help pay for the cost of receiving lessons or attending a summer music camp, etc. Most years we give out $1,000. Some years we've given two scholarships, $1,000 to one student, $500 to another. The students apply via our dear Anne Severy, who directs the MUHS Jazz Band, and we follow her lead/recommendation.

This scholarship has been so very meaningful for the many recipients who have received it since 2009, for some I might even say "life-changing." In an effort not to be too long in this email, I'm just going to tell you about this year's recipient, who will receive the scholarship in a few weeks. His name is Oziah Wales, and he is just finishing his sophomore year. What is extra special is that he knew and loved Dan! Oziah was in the first grade class in Weybridge where Dan was working as a classroom aide when he first got cancer (diagnosed during the summer of that year).

I ran into Oziah several years after Dan died. I introduced myself, and he told me Dan was his favorite teacher. They had a special connection. Oziah didn't even know Dan played and loved music, but Oziah grew up to become an incredibly gifted musician. He plays piano, organ, alto and tenor sax! This year we had him visit to try out Dan's tenor sax. It turns out Oziah's own tenor sax was starting to have some problems and so the timing could not have been more perfect for us to loan him (indefinitely) Dan's sax. He loves it. The night we gave it to him, Oziah's mom told me that when she went to say good night to him, she saw Oziah had put out on his desk a drawing Dan had made and given to him way back in first grade. Oziah had kept that drawing all these years. Several weeks ago we were able to go hear Oziah play in the All State Jazz Band up in Swanton, playing Dan's tenor sax! It sounded great, and we knew how happy Dan would be.

October–November, 2016

Dear Friends,

Surprise! Although my series of Dan letters has ended, here I am writing to you again. How is that?!? Maybe every now and then, a story will just come along that begs to be told. I tried resisting writing you about this one; some of you have already heard it anyway. But the story won out, and here I am writing it down.

I spent a lot of time this summer tending my flower gardens, much like last year. It was another dry one, so watering was an almost daily chore. One area of my yard I mentioned to you a few years back. It's the one I cleared with the help of the fellow called Dan. It sits between two tall pine trees and the edge of the brook. The pine trees were just skinny shoots when Gregg brought them home in the mid-1980s. The garden club was giving them away at the back of Ilsley Library. Now they are towering pines and two of my favorite trees on our property.

It was Gregg who suggested we think of them as representing our two boys. We probably planted them too close together, but I love the way they've grown to almost look like one huge pine. I remember when I was little playing under some pines in the wintertime. You could feel like you were hiding in a fort, with the soft, snow-laden branches wrapped over you like a blanketed roof. And

there's nothing quite like the sound of wind whispering through
pine branches, calling one to something nameless and beyond.
  Once this little area was cleared of bushes and poison ivy and
such, I waited to see what direction it might take. I did have a few
shrubs planted along the edge, mostly because that was as far in as
I could dig. But what to do in the middle area? I waited for inspi-
ration and a vision. And I waited some more.

> Do you have the patience to wait
> Till your mud settles and the water is clear?
> Can you remain unmoving
> Till the right action arises by itself?

> —Tao Te Ching

Over the next year, what grew up through the cardboard I'd
put down to discourage poison ivy, etc., were ferns. I'd no sooner
decided to call this new area "Fernglade" when a friend showed up
with a wrought iron chair. I'd previously admired her thrift-store
find, and she had decided it really just didn't work for her. She was
giving it to me. I said, "I know exactly where it will go!" You see,
the back of the chair is designed with ferns, so into "Fernglade" it
went. This is not a chair I sit in, but it is an important part of this
garden area. It is an invitation to the invisible guests.
  While digging and clearing this bit of land, I did come across
a few relics from decades past when the kids were little—broken
pieces from old toys and games, etc. This small collection sits
under a basswood tree near the chair. For me who moved every
four years growing up, it's especially sweet to have lived for so long
now in one place that remnants of our early family life become
unearthed every so often.
  Many little garden areas surround our house, and each one
seems to have a different personality or quality of presence. Some

are more subdued or shy. Others are quite brash, loud, and color-ful! Some are very resilient, others need more attention and care. I think of them rather like they are my children, or maybe just parts of myself? Sometimes an unhappy bush needs to be moved, or certain soil needs a boost of manure. I walk around them every day in the summer, watering and listening.

Back to Fernglade. There's nothing special to look at. And yet. For quite some time I have been aware of an energy there. Even before the pine needles drop to form a soft carpet, even before the brook dries up and stops its noisy babbling, there is a quality of stillness and peace. With the pine trees, the toy remnants, the chair inviting in the unseen, it seems a place for remembering. Remembering and giving thanks to the ancestors and for all that endures over time and generations. Fernglade feels somehow like a place where many paths have converged.

I have set the scene for you now, to bring to you to August 2016. As I've gotten older, I've been able to notice certain patterns to the ups and downs of my emotional life. In August, when the light starts to shift and the songs of the birds and insects change, too, there is a certain wistful poignancy in the air that is very beautiful but also stirs some uneasiness in me. It's that back-to-school time. As a teacher, I was always most anxious the weeks before school started. And remembering way back, there were the early years of my own going to school. I think our bodies store these memories.

This year, on August 20, I was feeling a little shaky. In the morning I ran errands and on two occasions told others about how I went away to an English boarding school on the island of Barbados when we were living on Tobago. It was such an exciting adventure, taking a plane to a separate island. But it was also a challenge, being so completely on one's own at age 10 and not seeing one's parents for several months. There were no peer support groups, counselors, or anyone to turn to. We really were on our own, except we slept 12 cots in a dorm! I like to say that's when my relationship with "God" really deepened, because for at least the first month, before I'd made a best friend, who else was there to talk to? And it is also when I became a letter writer. Letters were my umbilical cord to home (in those days—no communication via email or even telephone).

On this Saturday in August, after coming home from errands, I felt it was the day to make something in Fernglade. I had been thinking over several weeks that I needed a standing rock, as tall as I could find. I had some rocks on the far side of the garage left over from previous projects. One looked like it would be perfect, if I could somehow get it to Fernglade and turn it up on one end.

After much effort and carting more rocks than I'd intended, I ended with my tallest rock standing up and three others standing around the base to keep it secure. I can't properly express how good I felt! This physical exertion had completely changed my mood from one of mild anxiety to strength and groundedness. I loved the "sculpture" I'd ended up with. I called it my antenna to heaven. The transmission was clear. I felt connected and strong.

The next day I was reflecting some more on the unease I can feel in August. I remembered that besides the school separation anxiety, my mother had also died in August. When was that? I could not remember, so went looking for her obituary. I found it and read that she died on August 20, 1991. In fact, the day before, when I'd made the sculpture, it had been the 25th anniversary of her dying! Wow. Maybe that helped explain the "rightness" I had felt as I worked with those rocks, a force moving with and through me. I decided to dedicate the sculpture to "mother love"—the perfect antidote to the separation anxiety and homesickness I had felt so long ago.

I thought the sculpture was complete, but it was not. Maybe a week later I found myself wishing I'd had a large round rock as one of the supports. I did not have any large round rocks, but I did have some small round ones from Maine. After playing around *with some, I ended up balancing three of them on parts of the larger rocks. Three seemed just the right amount.*

More days went by. One morning as I was watering one of the azaleas, I looked up and was startled to see what my sculpture had become. The addition of the small round stones had made two of the larger rocks look like people. There before me, without a doubt, was "Mother and Child."

Another day as I approached Fernglade to water nearby azaleas, it looked to me as though Mother had moved. From one angle she looks like she is standing next to Child with the long sleeve of her robe down her side. But from this other angle, it looked to me like her arms were now up in front of her in a prayer pose! What!?! I shook my head. As I walked back inside wondering about this area in my yard, I heard a voice in my head say something like "It's a prayer point, silly!"

And so my relationship with this sculpture continues to deepen. It seems like a living sculpture because it changes. The smaller round stones fall off periodically and when I balance them back on top, they look slightly different each time. And there's also the changing light hitting the surface of the rocks. And when it rains, I suddenly have a dark Madonna and child.

One day it occurred to me that the number of rocks might be significant. There are four larger ones and three smaller round ones on top. I Googled seven and on the site I found information especially relevant. "Seven is the number of the Universe. It is the three of heavens (soul) combined with the four (body) of the earth...seven represents the virginity of the Great Mother, the feminine archetype—She who creates."

The most recent gift of the sculpture has been to remind me of a dream I had almost two years after Dan died. It was a very vivid dream, and in it Dan was a little boy about three or four. He was very happy, exuberant, and he was getting a big chuckle out of something that to me wasn't all that funny. Dan's quirky and silly sense of humor! But the best part of the dream was at one point we were walking, and his hand was in mine. And I could truly feel it. I woke from that dream in tears.

Dream experts suggest that we are all of the characters in our dreams. I wonder if this could be true, too, for the creations we make, like my statue. If so, then part of me is the mother, the child, and even the third entity in the sculpture, the littlest one who stands slightly behind, as witness consciousness.

Sometimes we travel far and wide in search of new vistas and inspiration. Sometimes we stay close to home. Whether you journey a distance or just out into your own backyard, may you feel nourished by all that is sacred and holy in this life of which we are blessed to be a part.

xxx Susan, Susie, Sue

P.S. Attached are a few quotes.

P.P.S. Recently I came across the plant tag to the bush that happens to be in front of my sculpture. It's an azalea. Its name is "A Heavenly Thing."

The real voyage of discovery consists not in seeking new landscapes but in having new eyes.
—Marcel Proust

If one completes the journey to one's own heart, one will find oneself in the heart of everyone else.
—Father Thomas Keating

THERE WERE SO MANY kindnesses after Dan died. One of them hangs in our bedroom. A local artist I knew only slightly invited

Natalie and me to visit her studio and pick out two of her works to bring home.

Natalie chose a pastel of a running brook. "Healing waters" is what I silently prayed. I looked for one I felt drawn to but also hoped was not worth too much. Artists tend to be generous, but they usually need all the money they can make. I ended up choosing one that was a rough sketch of a scene where the viewer is standing on a bluff and looking down and out to the ocean beyond. I believe the artist told me she drew it while attending a workshop in Maine, and she was missing her husband. There are two trees in the foreground with several shades of green for the leaves and a rich deep blue for the trunks, along with a vein of magenta. That same magenta, in a slightly lighter shade, shows up again as a mist on the horizon, where the water seems to disappear into the sky. Almost immediately, I imagined that Gregg and I were the trees, and we were waving goodbye to Dan, whose essence, the magenta mist, was now dissipating out into the world.

Much later I came to appreciate the name of the work, *Vantage Point*, which I found written on the back. The longer I live, the better I am able to come to terms with Dan's leaving and also to see how all the little moments over the years relate and start to form a bigger picture, puzzle pieces in a larger circle of connection and meaning.

Most of the time, I am content. I am at peace with how things are. And yet, there are moments, times when I pass a bicyclist on the road, or catch a glimpse of a young man from a certain angle, or notice the shape of a particular pair of hands. My heart leaps in recognition. After all these years, there is still residual disbelief, and a soul's yearning that will always be a part of who I am.

For the past three years my end-of-summer bouquets, gathered from the garden, have all gone to bring comfort to grieving friends whose husbands died unexpectedly. But this year is going to be different; Natalie is getting married! She has asked me if I would like to provide the flowers for the wedding. Natalie didn't really date or look for a relationship after Dan died; I think she was just too busy with her studies and work. But several years ago, she met a lovely man in a yoga class, and they are getting married in early August, 10 years after her marriage to Dan. This is a joyous event, yet one that is tinged with a sweet wistfulness, too. It's a big deal, another milestone on my path. I feel Dan with me; I feel his love and his total support of Natalie and her fiancé, John. And he is so pleased that I will be providing the flowers for the wedding!

Shortly after Dan died, Natalie found a book by Rilke on his bookshelf, a book he had likely read as part of the research for his senior thesis. When Natalie and I read it, we appreciated how Dan had underlined passages, sometimes adding a drawing or a comment.

I wish I had asked Dan what he made of Rilke. I wish I had asked permission to read his thesis. As I mentioned before, when Dan was a senior at Willamette University he started to experience some psychological difficulties. We were worried that he wouldn't be able to finish his thesis and thus might not graduate. I remember encouraging him not to worry about the grade, just get it done. Dan considered taking an antipsychotic drug a doctor had recommended, to help with his state of mind. In the end, Dan chose not to take anything, he completed his thesis, and even got an A on it. Over time, his inner turmoil and difficult mood swings softened, and Dan started to take pleasure in his life once again. I probably never asked Dan about Rilke because it seemed wise to leave well enough alone—to just be grateful he was back on an even keel.

I am planning to reread Dan's copy of Rilke's *Letters to a Young Poet*. There were things I did not fully understand the first time through. The last sentence Dan underlined in the book is, "In it I speak to you further of life and death and of how both are great and glorious." Below that, to the left of where Rilke signed his name at the end of that particular letter, Dan wrote, "Death is the completion of life."

While Dan's life was cut short by cancer, I believe that time is relative, and that he accomplished everything he came here to do. And we who knew him are blessed by that knowing. As for me, I have more to learn, and mysteries to ponder. My journey continues; as one particular path comes to a close, another opens and beckons me onward.

I have been writing this story for a long time. Or maybe it has been writing me? Whichever it is, I carry forward, like a lucky stone in my pocket, these words by Henri-Frederic Amiel:

> Life is short and we have
> never too much time for
> gladdening the hearts of
> those who are traveling
> the dark journey with us.
> Oh be swift to love, make
> haste to be kind.

May it be so.

The Monarch and the Ring

Although the plan was to pick the wedding flowers in the early evening, I found myself visiting the garden beds off and on throughout the afternoon. And that's when I noticed a change in the air, a stepping into sacred space. A peacefulness descended over our property like a holy mantle. And I saw my first monarch of the season.

Unlike ones I've seen in the past, this butterfly hung around our yard for a long time. It flew everywhere, not only landing on the zinnias I would soon be picking, but also flying up into trees, over the house, and swooping in and around Fernglade. I had been in somewhat of a serious mood; I knew we were on another threshold. I was being called to rise to the occasion and make Dan proud.

But watching this playful monarch zooming here and there, I almost laughed out loud! The lightness of being! And then I imagined Dan talking to me, through the butterfly. He said, "Mom, it's totally fine and normal for you to be feeling a bit sad and to be missing me. But please don't be sad for me. Because I am happy! Where I am now is so amazing!"

I remembered that Dan had suffered at the end of his life. He was weighed down. Now, wherever he was on the Other Side, he was free.

The wedding preparations began months in advance, with each detail carefully worked out. That's why I was so surprised when

Natalie called with a wedding question just five days before the ceremony. She was asking for our permission about something, though she needn't have. Apparently John had been to the local jewelry shop but still hadn't found a wedding band he liked. Natalie wondered if it would be all right with Gregg and me if she offered Dan's ring to John. Without a moment's hesitation I said, "Yes! Dan would love it if John liked his ring and wanted to wear it."

I teared up a few times during the following days. Not so much from sadness but from wonderment. I imagined the depth of Dan's love and generosity now that he exists as his Higher Self. I, on the other hand, am still in my limited human form. Half-jokingly I said to Dan, "Really? Now you have to give away your ring?" He said, "Absolutely, Mom."

I'd been wondering how Dan would bless this wedding, because I knew he surely would. I'd been thinking he would do so by helping me provide the flowers. But now, I could not imagine a more perfect gift than his ring.

Natalie sent me an email the next day: "It's such a special ring and holding it brings back a lot of memories and love. John tried it on and he does really like it. He was moved seeing it.... The ring will be a meaningful way to keep Dan near to both of our hearts, as well as a reminder of his love and protection, on our wedding day and always."

I took lots of photographs of the ceremony and reception, but there was really only one moment I just *had* to capture. And I did! It's a beautiful photograph of Natalie putting Dan's ring on John's finger. In this image, Monsignor stands between them, his hand hovering over theirs. And Dan, though invisible, is right there too, blessing this union and all that lies ahead.

ACKNOWLEDGMENTS

Many people helped bring this book into being. I am deeply grateful to you all.

Bianca Giaever typed the original handwritten letters. Mel Huff made minor edits and formatted the pages to prepare them for readers. Vanessa Wolff was a constant sounding board and she, Marianne Doe, Kris Butler, and Deb Cossaart critiqued the manuscript. Louise Watson proofread it several times, and she and Pat Goudey O'Brien advised, edited, and formatted the final manuscript. Diane Birnbaum and Lisa Vandermade assisted with artistic decisions. Dean Bornstein designed the book's pages and cover and prepared the manuscript for printing. Gregg Humphrey helped with various computer challenges and was a steady and calm support. And all of you were incredibly encouraging, helpful, and patient each step of the way.

Gratitude to Andy, Megan, Drew, Phoebe, and Hadley Humphrey for bringing joy into my life. And to Natalie Guarin, who always inspires.

Special thanks to David Foss, who believed in this work when it was just a seed of an idea. He edited, proofread, guided the permissions process, worked on the copyright, credits, and bibliography pages, and came up with the first cover design. I turned to him with all manner of questions and he lighted the way.

Finally, I wish to acknowledge all my friends who, with generous hearts, received and read these letters over many years. You told me to keep writing and I did. Thank you.

CREDITS

Bibliography

Andrews, Ted. *Animal Speak: The Spiritual & Magical Powers of Creatures Great & Small.* Woodbury, Minnesota: Llewellyn Publications, 1993.

Belletini, Mark. "Reading for the Day." *Sonata for Voice and Silence: Meditations.* Boston: Skinner House Books, 2008.

Brach, Tara, Ph.D. *True Refuge.* New York: Bantam Books, 2013.

Burnham, Sophy. *A Book of Angels: Reflections on Angels Past and Present, and True Stories of How They Touch Our Lives.* New York: Random House, 1990.

Burton, Virginia Lee. *The Little House.* Boston: Houghton Mifflin, 1969.

Chödrön, Pema. *The Places That Scare You: A Guide to Fearlessness in Difficult Times.* Boston: Shambhala Publications, 2002.

Gangaji. *The Diamond in Your Pocket: Discovering Your True Radiance.* Louisville, Colorado: Sounds True, 2007.

Greenspan, Miriam. *Healing Through the Dark Emotions: The Wisdom of Grief, Fear, and Despair.* Boston: Shambhala Publications, 2003.

Hanh, Thich Nhat. "No Coming, No Going." *You Are Here: Discovering the Magic of the Present Moment.* Boston: Shambhala Publications, 2009.

Hickman, Martha Whitmore. *Healing After Loss: Daily Meditations for Working Through Grief.* New York: HarperCollins, 2002.

Katie, Byron. *Loving What Is: Four Questions That Can Change Your Life.* New York: Three Rivers Press, 2002.

Leen, Jason. *The Death of the Prophet.* Bellevue, Washington: Illumination Arts, 1988.

Levertov, Denise. "The Avowal." *Oblique Prayers.* New York: New Directions, 1984.

Merwin, W.S. "Separation." *Migration: New and Selected Poems.* Port Townsend, Washington: Copper Canyon Press, 1963, 2005.

Newman, Marjorie, and Patrick Benson. *Mole and the Baby Bird.* New York: Bloomsbury, 2002.

Nye, Naomi Shihab. "Kindness." *Words Under the Words: Selected Poems.* Portland, Oregon: Far Corner Books, 1995.

O'Donohue, John. *Anam Cara: A Book of Celtic Wisdom.* New York: HarperCollins, 1997.

Oliver, Mary. *New and Selected Poems.* Boston: Beacon Press, 1993.

Oliver, Mary. "Invitation." *Red Bird.* Boston: Beacon Press, 2008.

O'Rourke, Meghan. "Good Grief." *The New Yorker,* January 24, 2010.

Rilke, Rainer Maria. *Letters to a Young Poet.* New York: Vintage Books, 1986.

Sarton, May. *Journal of a Solitude.* New York: W.W. Norton & Co., Inc., 1977.

Schwartz, Robert. *On Courageous Souls: Do We Plan Our Life Challenges Before Birth?* Chesterland, Ohio: Whispering Winds Press, 2007.

Scott-Maxwell, Florida. *The Measure of My Days*. New York: Penguin Books, 1979.

Siegel, Daniel J., M.D. *Mindsight: The New Science of Personal Transformation*. New York: Bantam Books, 2010.

Simon, Tami. Interview with Tara Brach on "Tara Brach: Radical Acceptance." *Insights at the Edge*. Originally broadcast August 13, 2013. Louisville, Colorado: Sounds True.

Soros, Barbara, and Danuta Mayer. *Tenzin's Deer: A Tibetan Tale*. Cambridge, Massachusetts: Barefoot Books, 2003.

Tagore, Rabindranath. "Peace, My Heart." *The Gardener*. New York: The Macmillan Company, 1913.

Taylor, Jill Bolte, Ph.D. *My Stroke of Insight: A Brain Scientist's Personal Journey*. New York: Penguin Books, 2009.

Walcott, Derek. "Love After Love." *The Poetry of Derek Walcott 1948–2013*. New York: Farrar, Straus and Giroux, 2014.

CPSIA information can be obtained
at www.ICGtesting.com
Printed in the USA
LVHW041719231020
669518LV00003B/224